Collared

Collared

Politics and Personalities in Oregon's Wolf Country

Aimee Lyn Eaton

Oregon State University Press • Corvallis

The paper in this book meets the guidelines for permanence and durability of the Committee on Production Guidelines for Book Longevity of the Council on Library Resources and the minimum requirements of the American National Standard for Permanence of Paper for Printed Library Materials Z39.48-1984.

Library of Congress Cataloging-in-Publication Data

Eaton, Aimee Lyn.
  Collared : politics and personalities in Oregon's wolf country / Aimee Lyn Eaton.
     pages cm
  Includes bibliographical references and index.
  ISBN 978-0-87071-706-2 (alk. paper) -- ISBN 978-0-87071-707-9 (e-book)
1. Wolves--Oregon. 2. Wolves--Control--Oregon. 3. Wolves--Conservation--Oregon. I. Title. II. Title: Politics and personalities in Oregon's wolf country. III. Title: Oregon's wolf country.
  QL737.C22E18 2013
  599.77309795--dc23

                    2013013092

Oregon State University Press

121 The Valley Library
Corvallis OR 97331-4501
541-737-3166 • fax 541-737-3170
www.osupress.oregonstate.edu

For Mike

Table of Contents

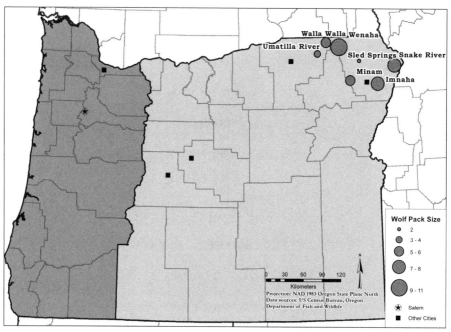

The Cascade Mountain Range separates Oregon by geography, climate, population, and some would say politics. This divide has played a major role in both the public perception, and the management, of wolves in the state.

Map created by James Duncan, Research Specialist, University of Vermont

Introduction

On the last Thursday in April 2012, the Wallowa County Chamber of Commerce hosted a community meeting titled Wolves II: Know the Facts. Perhaps due to the weather, which was cold, blustery, and threatening snow, or perhaps because it was a school night and also calving season, the meeting failed to gather the standing-room-only crowds for which the region and topic have become known. Instead a small group comprising mostly families complete with grandparents and children spread across the back rows of the chamber's business center.

After a flag salute for which all the attendees stood, covered their hearts, and recited the Pledge of Allegiance, Fred Steen moved to the front of the room. He stood with feet shoulder-width apart, hands clasped behind his back, handgun holstered at his side. Steen is not a wildlife biologist. He is not a rancher. He did not have a PowerPoint presentation or any handouts. Yet he talked about wolves and their impact within the county for almost an hour. He was at attention the entire time. He is the Wallowa County sheriff.

"A number of livestock producers were dissatisfied with the Oregon Department of Fish and Wildlife," said Steen. "The cattlemen felt their needs and issues were not being represented and they were upset. I was approached in 2010 by a few different producers and asked to assist with management and issues of potential depredation. After considering the situation, the sheriff's office decided wolves are a public concern, and this is an issue of keeping the peace."

Following that decision, Steen and his office began to treat any potential wolf activity as criminal. "We set up a method by which when there was a suspected depredation the livestock producer had the option of calling the sheriff, USDA Wildlife Services, or ODFW [Oregon Department of Fish and Wildlife]. The goal was to create a specific and directed protocol," said Steen. "We go in and let the evidence take us where it will, and we maintain control of that evidence whatever it may be. We make sure carcasses are properly handled and frozen and retain possible genetic material for the labs to analyze."

Speaking to the group, Steen recalled a phone conversation from early in the month with a woman who suspected a wolf had been on her property and wished to file a police report, a common and encouraged move. She had let her five-year-old son and their malamute out to play in the yard, said Steen. Fifteen minutes later the boy came back inside visibly shaken and upset, telling his mother there was a monster near the house, and the dog had run off. The woman sat her young son down and showed him a variety of images depicting coyotes, dogs, and wolves in the wild. The boy pointed to an image of a wolf. Steen took the woman's statement and filed it in his office alongside the dozens of other wolf-related reports that had been recorded in the last two years. In the case against wolves, the more documented information the better, said Steen.

Five-year-olds identifying monsters seen at more than fifty yards, dead cows being cordoned off in fields and their remains stuffed in cold storage, samples of potential wolf DNA being sent to university forensic labs: from an outside perspective this can seem like hysteria. Given historical context, however, it becomes a pattern.

For hundreds of years humans have been afraid of wolves. They've feared being attacked in the night, their children being dragged off, their livestock eaten. They've imagined wolves as the devil's dogs, eyes glowing yellow, teeth dripping as they guard the gates of hell. They've told their children stories of the Big Bad Wolf who ate Grandma, the wolf who will huff and puff and blow the house down, and the wolf in sheep's clothing. The resulting historical manifestation of these caricatures was the widespread hunting and killing of wolves throughout much of Europe during the Middle Ages and in the United States as the New World was populated by Europeans.

There is little doubt that American colonists brought their stigma against wolves with them into the new territories. As wolves killed domestic animals important to human survival, conflict between early settlers and wolves became unavoidable. The first official wolf bounty was set in 1630 in Plymouth Colony. Other bounties followed and within the century, wolves had been exterminated from New England. As settlers expanded westward they furthered their attempts to remove wolves from the landscape; however, the gross number of wolves outpaced the number of successful hunts, and for more than two hundred years wolves continued to roam across undeveloped and developing landscapes. Then in 1913, after pioneers in the western territories had filed numerous and ongoing complaints with the federal government about livestock losses due to animal attacks, Congress delegated all predator control to the U.S. government under the Division of Predator and Rodent Control. The mandate placed wolves officially on the US government's most-wanted list, and federally employed hunters were paid to track, kill, and eradicate the species.

At the time of the ruling's enactment wolves were found throughout Oregon. Packs covered territory to the east and west of the Cascade Range and from the Washington to California borders, but once predator control received official sanction, it took just thirty-three years for every last wolf in the state to be found and killed. The eradication lasted until 1999, when the recovery of wolves in Oregon was prompted by the earlier enactment of the federal Endangered Species Act and the development of active management programs for wolves within specified regions of the continental United States.

The first wolf to reenter Oregon was originally part of a population of gray wolves reintroduced into Idaho from Canada by the United States Fish and Wildlife Service (USFWS). After only a few weeks, Oregon decided it was not ready to take on management of the species and deported the young wolf back to Idaho via helicopter. The move was later discovered to be in violation of the Endangered Species Act, but at the time the understanding of wolf management in the West was still in its infancy. In the years since that first incident, wolves have been allowed to return to Oregon. Yet that allowance has remained a subject of great debate and contention.

The almost innate fear of wolves cultivated during the Middle Ages still exists in many communities, especially those heavily dependent on livestock production like the small ranching towns in the northeast corner of the state. In these areas conflict between wolves and humans arose during the early stages of wolf reestablishment and has yet to abate. Disagreements regarding management coupled with changes to wolves' federal protection status have sparked widespread confusion about who, if anyone, is in charge of wolves within the state. "Liberal environmentalists" have squared off against "conservative ranchers" and both sides have stooped to name-calling and finger-pointing in efforts to get their points across.

Livestock producers have been issued shoot-to-kill permits to protect their livestock, while at the same time Oregon Department of Fish and Wildlife (ODFW) officials have had their ability to control problem wolves through lethal measures revoked by the State Court of Appeals. The state's wolf management plan has been continually critiqued, reevaluated, and ignored. Wolves have been removed from federal protection in the only areas of the state they inhabit. They have been fitted with radio collars for tracking purposes, caught in leg traps, tranquilized with darts shot from helicopters, shocked with electric currents, subjected to deterrent hazing measures, and killed outright. Yet still the wolf population grows.

At the close of 2012, state officials counted seven distinct wolf packs in Oregon, totaling at least forty-six wolves. Most of these animals are rarely seen by humans, but ODFW biologists have seen their prints in the mud and their scat on the trails. They've heard them howling at night and have succeeded in recording the yips of pups and the deeper baritones of adults. In an effort to keep better tabs on the population, state biologists have attempted to place radio or GPS collars on an animal or two from each known pack. Using information downloaded from the collars, managers have found that wolves generally range over low-elevation private lands during the winter and spring—a time that coincides with cattle being held at home and calving season—and over higher-elevation public lands during the summer, when cattle are put out to graze. The ODFW has shared this information with the ranching community and has incorporated new technologies to alert livestock producers about when wolves are in close proximity to grazing lands. This information sharing has been good for relations but has done little to reduce fear.

Between May 5, 2010, and September 1, 2012, the ODFW confirmed twenty-nine livestock deaths that were attributable to wolves. These weren't simple, clean kills. The carcasses of young calves and postpartum cows were found ripped to shreds on private lands, their bodies half consumed. The loss of these domestic animals represents real economic hardship for ranching families that have long supported their communities, and the trickle-down effect can be seen in the number of small businesses and townspeople who are increasingly vocal in their opposition to wolves.

In the same meeting at which Sheriff Fred Steen spoke about treating livestock depredations as crime scenes, the chamber's executive director, Vicki Searles, said, "You would be hard-pressed to find someone in support of wolves in Wallowa County. There are a few of them out there, but they're closeted. It's the ranchers who support this area, and to come out for wolves is to come out against your neighbors. In a community as tight-knit as Wallowa not many people are willing to do that."

The same cannot be said for many of the areas west of the Cascade Range. In the heavily populated areas surrounding Eugene, Salem, and Portland, support for wolves is much easier to find. Regional conservation groups have mobilized the public around reestablishment of wolves, providing opportunities for schoolchildren to participate in art projects about wolves and creating competitions to give the animals names that are more personable than the letter-number combinations used by the state. Many of these same groups have banded together to take the state of Oregon to court over its management of wolves, claiming the 2005 wolf conservation and management plan developed by the ODFW in collaboration with numerous different stakeholder groups violates the state's endangered species law and therefore renders the plan void.

"We feel that the problem is the management and the community, not the wolves," says Nick Cady, a lawyer for Cascadia Wildlands, a group based in Eugene, Oregon, that is one of the three involved in the lawsuit. "We are looking to create incentives to encourage responsible ranching so that wolf populations may continue to grow and distribute throughout Oregon."

The majority of Oregonians want to protect wolves, says Cady, and that's tentatively true. Ten years before wolves began to reestablish populations in the state, a 1999 poll of five hundred randomly selected Oregonians that was commissioned by the Oregon Natural Desert Association (ONDA) and paid for by ONDA, Defenders of Wildlife, the Oregon Natural Resources Council, and the Predator Defense Institute found that 70 percent of Oregonians supported the return of wolves to Oregon. What the poll didn't ask, and what Cady doesn't say, is at what cost?

The majority of Oregonians, including Cady, have never been out to Wallowa County. They haven't met the ranchers or attended the community meetings where fear of wolves seems to run as wild as the wolves themselves. Wolf sign has not been found on their property, and they haven't had to absorb the monetary loss that comes with the death of a livestock animal. This lack of intimacy isn't by itself a failing, but just as a misunderstanding of conservation goals and ethics may impact how ranching communities perceive those wishing to protect wolves, it has the potential to result in misinterpretations and unjust conclusions that may negatively impact overall recovery efforts.

While the population of wolves in Oregon may never realize the numbers seen in Idaho and Montana, where the estimated number of wolves has crept to 746 and 566, respectively, there is little doubt that wolves will gain a hold here. In Oregon the wolf population is currently only slightly greater than the number of students in many urban classrooms, yet scientific models and agency predictions suggest the population will experience continued growth, with dispersal occurring across the state. This may be frightening on both sides of the debate. Those opposed to wolves see their continued growth as a pathway to potential economic ruin and loss of their livelihood and way of life. Those in favor fear the persecution and murder of wolves, and a continued loss of wildness.

When it comes down to it, when all the rhetoric is washed away and all the opinions and fears temporarily swept under the rug, wolves are wild animals, like mountain lions and bears, bobcats and coyotes. Just as the humans involved in the wolf debate deserve to be seen as individuals, not stereotypes, so do the wolves. They are not the boogeyman, or storybook monsters aiming to prey upon the young and old. They aren't cuddly pets or religious icons. They are *Canis lupus*. Wolves.

Wolves in Oregon

"There will likely be something going on this week. Come on out."

Famous last words.

It's 5:45 a.m. on the second to last Wednesday in May 2012, and I'm sitting in the parking lot of the Starbucks in La Grande, Oregon, waiting on a text message from the state's wolf coordinator, Russ Morgan. Morgan had invited me to make the seven-hour drive out from the Willamette Valley to the northeast corner of state this week because Oregon Department of Fish and Wildlife (ODFW) researchers were actively trapping for wolves, and I'd asked to tag along during a radio-collaring operation. This is my third day of waiting, and after a couple of cold nights sleeping in the back of the truck, I'm impatient.

The message finally comes in at 8:15. It's two words: No wolves. I shake my head and crawl into the bed of the truck to try to get a little more sleep. Don't these animals know I'm trying to work?

No. No, they don't.

A week later, the ODFW has yet to trap a wolf. Instead of continuing to wait, Morgan has offered to take me into the field on an exploratory mission. I meet him at the eastern Oregon field office and begin loading backpacks and cameras into a white state-owned four-wheel-drive truck that we're taking for the day. Morgan places a box of gallon-sized Ziploc bags and an antenna that looks like the bunny ears that once sat on almost every television in America into the backseat of the truck. I raise my eyebrows at the Ziplocs, but the bunny ears are no surprise.

Two months earlier Morgan had captured a male wolf from Oregon's Wenaha pack and fitted him with a radio collar and GPS locator. The wolf, named OR-12 because he was the twelfth wolf to be collared in Oregon, had then been released and the ODFW had used data downloaded from the collar to track his movements. After information was gathered for a month, a digital map of the Wenaha territory showed that OR-12 had been daily leaving and returning to a single origin point. On Morgan's computer screen the wolf's pattern resembled an asterisk. Morgan suspected the center of the star might be the den site for the Wenaha pack. Our plan was to head into the field to find out if his suspicion was correct.

By using the antennae to track OR-12's radio collar from the field, Morgan would be able to determine roughly where OR-12 was in relation to us, and to the suspected den site. The Ziplocs are for collecting scat samples. I ask about the necessity of the gallon size, and it's Morgan's turn to raise his eyebrows. His expression seems to say, "Oh, just you wait." Morgan took his current position with the ODFW in 2007, as wolves were first coming into the state from Idaho and establishing territories in Union and Wallowa Counties. He's been dealing with wolf shit ever since; the scat samples are just the simplest form.

Trained as a field biologist, Morgan is one of a handful of state and federal employees nationwide who are on the front lines of wolf management. The job is rare because wolves are rare, and the men and women who work to manage wolves seem to be either idealists or gluttons for punishment. Maybe both.

In the cab of the truck Morgan tells me that of all the wolf program managers in the West, not a single one has lasted in their position for more than ten years. "It's thankless and it never stops," says Morgan. "It impacts your entire life. Health, relationships, all of it. Many of the western managers have had their marriages fall apart, largely due to the stress of the work. It follows you home." If history is a bellwether for the future, Morgan is about halfway through his tenure as a state wolf manager. In the driver's seat of the truck he is slumped slightly forward with his arms crossed over the top of the steering wheel. His mustache and beard are flecked with gray, and despite his apparent overall health he seems to have a weariness that goes beyond not getting enough sleep.

There are other predatory species in the West. There are other animals that make humans nervous, or that need special conservation strategies. Mountain lion, grizzly, salmon, spotted owl. They've all brought conflict, but it's nothing compared to what is happening with wolves, said Morgan, dragging a hand down his face. Wolves have been idolized and demonized with almost no middle ground. The result has been huge swings in both wolf populations and management philosophies. According to Morgan, managing wolves should not be excessively different from managing other wild animals—they all simply follow what their biology tells them to do. However, the human conflict and emotion surrounding wolves is increasingly unpredictable and constantly shifting with current events and politics. "Wolves have brought about a level of emotion and involvement from people outside wildlife management that is incomparable to what I've seen with any other animal," said Morgan.

The United States has a torrid history of wolf management. After European settlement, wolves were managed under the jurisdiction of the federal Predator Control Act, which sought their widespread extermination largely through poison and gunshot. With these methods, the last wolf in Oregon was killed in 1946 for a twenty-dollar bounty. The passage of the federal Endangered Species Act (ESA) in 1973 and the subsequent listing of the gray wolf as endangered throughout the contiguous United States and Mexico[1] brought an end to the kill-based management style but left large questions about how predator management should occur in the West. In 1980, the US Fish and Wildlife Service (USFWS) signed the Northern Rocky Mountain Wolf Recovery Plan, which recommended reintroducing gray wolves in central Idaho and Yellowstone National Park. The recommendation was a required part of the USFWS's compliance efforts with ESA recovery mandates for wolves, yet it took fifteen years for the initial stages of the plan to be implemented in the form of the relocation of sixty-six gray wolves from southwestern Canada to the States—thirty-one to Yellowstone and thirty-five to Idaho.

Carter Niemeyer was one of the government trappers involved in the original capture and relocation measures. Working with a team of biologists and "ornery" trappers living in Alberta, Canada, Niemeyer located more than seventeen different wolf packs that he considered capable of absorbing the removal of individuals for reintroduction purposes without ill effect. "Our goal was to capture wolves from several different packs so that the reintroduced population would be genetically diverse," said Niemeyer, who has worked with both federal and state agencies to manage wolves in the West. "By trapping animals from different territories that weren't closely related we hoped to provide the best opportunity for success within the reintroduced population."

Niemeyer's time spent tracking and culling individual animals from the different packs seems to have paid off. In the seventeen years since reintroduction in the northern Rocky Mountain recovery area, which includes Idaho, Montana, Wyoming, the easternmost portions of Washington and Oregon, and a small part of north-central Utah, those 66 wolves have increased their numbers to more than 1,174, comprising 287 packs and 109 breeding pairs.[2] The majority of these wolf packs have remained in Montana and Idaho near the areas where they were originally introduced. However, territory expansion and other biological tendencies have resulted in wolves moving into Oregon and Washington.

The process by which wolves leave their natal packs and either join other packs or establish new territory elsewhere is called dispersal. It's a common occurrence in wolf populations and is counted on in state and federal recovery plans as a mechanism for the natural reestablishment of wolves across geographic territories. According to renowned wolf biologist David Mech, most wolves disperse from their natal packs at the onset of sexual maturity. Any wolf born into a pack and not taking over a breeding position will eventually leave it, usually between and eleven and twenty-four months of age. "Each wolf pack can be viewed as a 'dispersal pump' that converts prey into young wolves and spews them far and wide over the landscape," wrote Mech. "A thriving pack of three to nine members producing six pups each year thus 'pumps out' about half its members annually." [3]

Not accounting for mortality, that sort of reproduction and the subsequent exodus results in an approximate doubling of the wolf population every two years. Because wolves are territorial and are also habitat generalists able to survive almost anywhere, the natural expansion into new unpopulated regions by dispersing wolves is largely a given. That's been a hard pill to swallow for communities already nervous about the prospect of wolves in their states. "One of the most common misconceptions people have about wolves in Oregon is that they were brought here in the back of trucks," said Morgan. "The state did not actively reintroduce wolves. They dispersed here of their own volition and on their own time frame."

The distance a dispersing wolf travels varies by the individual wolf and by the surrounding conditions at the time of dispersal. Some wolves will travel to the edge of their natal pack's territory and attempt to establish themselves as a neighbor. Others will travel hundreds of miles into areas without other wolves before settling down. Regardless of how far they travel, all dispersing wolves are looking for three things necessary for their survival: a mate, food, and defensible territory. According to Mech, there are a few ways a dispersing wolf can meet these needs: he can kill and replace the dominant wolf of an already established pack; he can join a pack briefly and try to lure out a female who will then move with him into new territory; or he can leave occupied territory, locate a mate doing the same thing, and together they can set up house in a new area that will ultimately expand the entire population's range. All options are risky, and the route chosen by any individual depends largely on the population's overall density within its range. If the population has already filled all the readily available space, dispersers have little option but to join established packs, often temporarily, or challenge pack leaders for a more permanent place within the pack. However, when a population is reestablishing and there are large areas that are not part of an established pack's range, it becomes much more likely that individuals will attempt to start new packs in areas that have long been without wolves.

The first wolf to reenter Oregon, a female yearling dubbed B-45 by wildlife managers, dispersed from the Jureano pack in central Idaho. Fording the Snake River, she crossed the Hells Canyon Wilderness and went into the wilderness of northeastern Oregon's Blue Mountains in early spring 1999. Because she was wearing a radio collar, researchers from both Idaho and Oregon were able to track B-45's movements with relative ease. Word of her arrival in Oregon spread rapidly through government agencies, and then out to the media and the public. In general, the news that for the first time in more than fifty years a living wolf was present in Oregon was not well received, and discussions on what was to become of B-45 could be heard throughout the state's capitol building, on the editorial pages of local and regional newspapers, at coffee shops, and in the ivory halls of the state's universities.

B-45 was protected under the federal Endangered Species Act and under Oregon's state ESA.[4] However, the state did not have a management plan capable of providing insight into how protection should occur, and officials claimed they were ill equipped to deal with wolves in the state. In a move that is now known to have been illegal under the federal ESA, state officials made the decision to relocate B-45 back to the designated wolf management areas in Idaho. For two days a small plane and helicopter worked in tandem to flush the young wolf out of the steep, forested wilderness of the Blue Mountains and into an open clearing where she could safely be captured. They eventually succeeded, and she was sedated, given a physical, and transported back across state lines.

B-45 seemed to recover relatively quickly from the experience. A month after her release she was seen north of McCall, Idaho, where she and a male wolf were thought to be establishing territory for a new pack.[5] The interest, some of it from national and international levels, that accompanied B-45 into Oregon and then back to Idaho was a harbinger of the political circus that would ensue as the wolf population continued to grow and expand at a rate much faster than anticipated.

At the time of reintroduction in 1995, federal and western wildlife managers thought it would likely take at least a decade before wolves began to expand out of the predefined management areas in Idaho and Montana. It was assumed that wolves, like most endangered species, were a fragile population in the West and it would take time to see them rebound in areas of reintroduction. However, like many assumptions, this was largely incorrect. "The reintroduced population was far more prolific and resilient than I ever would have anticipated," said Niemeyer. "At first we were handling every situation with kid gloves. We treated every wolf as if it was one precious commodity in the recovery effort. We realized pretty quickly that when left to its own devices the population had an amazing ability to adapt to new areas and circumstances." This was a realization that had managers in the region shifting rapidly from hoping they could keep enough animals alive to foster recovery to worrying about what an expanding wolf population meant for other species and the greater landscape.

At six months old, wolf pups need as many calories as adults, about six thousand per day. In packs that have yearling wolves in addition to a breeding pair and a litter of pups, resource demands can increase by a factor of fifteen, according to Mech. In terms of the gross amount of food necessary for a pack of six, this translates to about forty-three pounds of food necessary to feed the pack per day.[6] This means that when establishing territory, a breeding pair must select and defend an area much larger than what they require to sustain only themselves. As the wolf population increases, the number of individual territories also increases, yet the average size of each territory decreases.

During the early 2000s the growing wolf population in Idaho and Montana resulted in increased competition over food resources and breeding space. Associated conflict led to higher rates of dispersal, the splitting of packs, and the carving out of new territories by wolves establishing new packs. It wasn't long before the landscape of reintroduction neared saturation. Like B-45 before them, dispersing wolves began exploring new areas farther from their home packs, occasionally over state lines. Again, as was the case with B-45, their movements were followed carefully by people from all walks of life and in all positions of power.

First Meetings

Morgan is driving in low gear. Half his body is hanging out the truck's open window, and his eyes are fixed on the small weedy ditch that runs alongside what at one time might have been a logging road. It has been sprinkling on and off, and while the road is dry the ditch is still muddy. Small pools of standing water dusted with yellow pollen attract puddling butterflies slurping valuable minerals out of the algal-tinged slurry. Morgan leans a little farther out the window, then without hitting the brakes he reaches over and shifts the truck into park. Morgan's out of the truck before we're at a full stop, and I'm left staring out the open driver's door. I can just see the top of his head as he crouches in the ditch.

I push my own door open, scrambling out and around the front of the truck to sink down next to Morgan. Clearly embedded in the soft mud is a paw print. Two feet away is another. Reaching out toward the first print I spread my pinkie and thumb in the classic surfing "hang loose" sign. With my fingers I span the print from the toes to the back of the pad, and then again just below the small toe indentations. The whole print is roughly four inches long by about three inches wide. "That's a front foot," says Morgan, nodding at the print. He scans the ditch. "There's a hind print, and see over here there's a track going the other direction. This is a wolf highway." I stare at the ground, suddenly seeing prints everywhere. They look like dog prints but bigger, as if

Fido had hit a growth spurt in the middle of the night.[1] There in the ditch with my butt inches from the mud, it hits me. There are wolves in Oregon.

There exist two types of understanding: logical and emotional. Logically I had known wolves were in the state for years. They were regularly in the headlines of the biggest newspapers, and I'd been talking regularly with biologists and wildlife managers about their presence. Yet emotionally I didn't understand their presence until the physical proof of their existence was directly in front of me. The tracks were irrefutable.

We get back in the truck and continue up the road, stopping often to look at more tracks and to scoop large piles of reeking black wolf shit into the Ziplocs. We fold the bags over our hands, just like the signs at the dog park illustrate, and hold our breath as we gather the samples. It takes me only one pile to realize why the gallon size is necessary.

Eventually we reach a point where the tracks seem to leave the road. Morgan pulls out the bunny-ear antennae and listens for the beeps that signal the alpha wolf's presence. We hear a few muted beeps, but they're headed away from our intended direction and us. Morgan stashes the antenna in the truck and tells me if I need to pee I should do it here near the road. We shoulder our packs and walk into the undergrowth. It is just after noon. The sky is bright blue. Birds are chirping. I want to ask Morgan if he has a gun and if I should be afraid, but I don't. Instead I keep him in sight and try not to step on every stick in the forest.

We hike for fifteen minutes ducking under low branches and skirting around large fallen logs, their trunks rotten and crumbling. We cross a small creek and Morgan points out the game trails branching away from the small pools like spokes on a wagon wheel. We each follow a distinct trail but when I spot a clump of fur stuck in the thorns I stage whisper his name and wave the downy clump in the air for him to see. A minute later Morgan gestures for me to join him in the shadows at the edge of a small clearing. I breathe quietly through my mouth as I approach. Thirty yards away a pile of abandoned logs is in full sunlight. At one point probably fifty years earlier, loggers had come through the area felling trees and hauling them out to the road for transport to the mills in La Grande and Baker City, but for one reason or another they had left this pile behind. Portions of some of the logs had been eaten away and hollowed out by weather and insects, but a flash of movement at one end of the pile shows the trees did not go to waste.

It is 12:30. I touch Morgan's elbow and point. A small gray female pup,[2] still fluffy and round, has come out from one of the hollow logs. Neither Morgan nor I breathe. The pup moves farther into the clearing and gives a sharp puppy's bark. A male littermate appears. Morgan and I make our way around the clearing to a position where we can see the entrance to the den. Mosquitoes buzz around my shoulders as I crouch in the long grass fifty feet from the pups. Morgan pulls out a video camera. I click away with my camera, cursing the sound of the shutter release. Another pup appears and steps briefly into the sunlight before returning to the den. The gray pup and her brother soon follow.

We don't move. The grass in the clearing is littered with the bleached white remnants of deer scapulae and rib bones. Morgan points out spots where roughhousing pups or napping adults have pushed the grass flat. An upwind breeze brings a slight smell of decay. Still we wait.

The gray pup and three black pups move to stand in the shadows at the mouth of the den. They seem to be searching the clearing before they again retreat into the darkness. After a moment Morgan takes two pieces of bone and rubs them against one another producing scraping, knocking sounds. There is no response, and he repeats the noise. Still the pups remain hidden. The mosquitoes have progressed to biting through my cotton shirt, and I can see several on Morgan's face.

It is 12:35, and a full-grown black wolf is standing directly across from me at the edge of the clearing. From where he's sitting Morgan can't see her, and without turning, without moving, I whisper at him, "There's an adult!" She stares straight at me. Ten seconds go by. Thirty. A minute. Then she turns and is gone. Almost immediately a series of howls erupts. First from the direction in which the female disappeared, then seemingly from all around the clearing, the voices of the Wenaha wolf pack ping-pong like supermarket bouncy balls. The cacophony goes on for several minutes. When it quiets Morgan gestures and we rise and make our way back to the truck.

Driving back down the overgrown road, Morgan spots a white-headed woodpecker flying between trees. Pulling over, he trains a pair of field binoculars halfway up the red bark of a massive ponderosa pine. The bird is designated a Critical Species in Oregon due to habitat loss, and he hasn't seen one of the striking black woodpeckers with a white head and throat in several years. Though he's a scientist trained in fact and analysis, Morgan takes it as a much-needed good omen. An omen he's been waiting on for more than a decade.

Before the mid-1990s reintroduction in Yellowstone and Idaho, wolves weren't a regular topic of public conversation in the West, especially not in Oregon. After B-45's appearance in 1999 and the subsequent sightings of other wolves in the state, wolves began to make regular headlines. Their notoriety grew rapidly, and without any proof that wolves would be a problem in Oregon, many residents began to cry out for the removal of the species.

By 2002, still well before wolves had been irrefutably documented in Oregon, state wildlife managers had organized a series of fourteen town hall meetings throughout the state to let residents voice their concerns and opinions about the natural reestablishment of wolf populations. The meetings were held in November and December and in the months leading up to them scientists and policy makers at the ODFW had heard from a range of experts about what the arrival of wolves might mean for the state. "There was an understanding among the department that wolves would be in Oregon much sooner than had originally been anticipated," said Craig Ely, the ODFW's northeast regional manager at the time of the meetings. "The town hall meetings were an opportunity for us to share educational information with the public, and also a time for us to hear the concerns of Oregonians related to wolves. There were a lot of concerns."

Each of the town hall meetings opened with an introductory presentation by ODFW staff about the history of wolves in Oregon, their biology, and their migration into the state. This was followed by a facilitated period for oral public comments. Written comments were also accepted at the door. Similar community meetings on more benign topics often garnered an audience of ten or fewer. At the end of the two months of wolf meetings, more than 2,000 people had attended a session. They had submitted 1,600 oral comments and another 1,400 in writing. Four hundred questions had been asked and hundreds of pages of handouts had been distributed. It was an unprecedented response. "These meetings were held at dinnertime on weeknights," said Ely, who is now retired but still living within a stone's throw of the La Grande field office. "For so many people to take time out of their evenings, away from chores, families, and other commitments in order to come out and have their voices heard was something we'd never seen before." Besides setting turnout records, the town hall meetings did something else very important: they alerted state officials to the level of interest and objections that surrounded wolves.

From the get-go it was clear that wolves were going to be a contentious topic, said Ely. After the meetings there was no doubt that the state needed to start planning for how it was going to address the issues surrounding wolves well before there was a viable population in Oregon. Waiting for the wolves to arrive was not an option.

Building on the momentum of the town hall meetings, the state's Fish and Wildlife Commission approved a process to develop a wolf management and conservation plan. The process called for the organization of a fourteen-member Wolf Advisory Committee (WAC) made up of public stakeholders from different walks of life. By proactively working to create a plan for wolves that incorporated a diverse array of viewpoints, the commission hoped to have a handle on management and its potential pitfalls before wolves made Oregon home.

The WAC would meet once a month from November 2003 to December 2004. Appointment to the committee would be based on nomination and would take into account an individual's background, a statement about why the individual was qualified to sit on the committee, what perspective the individual might lend to the committee, the individual's willingness to partake in the planning process, and the individual's residency status.

On June 6, 2003, after reviewing 134 nomination letters for 82 individual nominees, the commission appointed the following 14 people to the WAC, representing specific geographic locations and stakeholder groups:[3]

Sandy Sanderson, Salem, OR, hunters
Sharon Beck, Cove, OR, livestock producers
Meg Mitchell, Enterprise, OR, public lands manager
Joe Colver, Portland, OR, trappers
Ben Boswell, Enterprise, OR, eastern Oregon county commissioners
Brett Brownscombe, La Grande, OR, range and forest conservationists
Bob Lund, La Grande, OR, citizens-at-large
Bill Gawloski, Silverton, OR, citizens-at-large
Dan Edge, Corvallis, OR, educators
Bob Riggs, La Grande, OR, wildlife biologists and researchers
Hans Radtke, Yachats, OR, economists
Clint Krebs, Ione, OR, rural Oregon residents
Ken Hall, Pendleton, OR, Native American tribes
Amaroq Weiss, Ashland, OR, wolf conservationists

Read that list again. Don't concentrate too much on the names of the individuals, yet. Instead look at the towns and notice the splits between the east and west side of the state. Then look at the groups that were represented. There were ranchers, environmentalists, politicians, and academics. They came from the state's largest population center, and some of its smallest towns.[4] Before the meetings ever started, the committee members had vast differences in how they viewed the world and the way they lived their lives. Despite this, the group, with the assistance of Mark Henjum, the ODFW eastern regional biologist in charge of special projects, and Paul De Morgan, an independent meeting facilitator, was charged with determining how the state would respond to wolves for the foreseeable future.

To defuse potential conflict within the group before the meetings were underway, the commission laid out one primary statement, said De

Morgan, who went on to mediate the process behind Washington State's wolf management plan. "To some extent the commission had already experienced and dealt with a lot of aggression and conflict during the town hall meetings, so they were aware that there was a potential for more conflict than conversation with the WAC," said De Morgan. "To mitigate this they set the expectation that wolves coming into Oregon was unavoidable and nonnegotiable. Therefore the WAC wasn't responsible for answering the question of 'Should there be wolves in Oregon?' but rather for determining a plan as to how the state should manage for wolves when they got here."

With that dictum in mind, the WAC was given ten months and told to come back with a plan.

Getting Organized

There are twenty-one milk crate–sized boxes of documents stacked like building blocks along the back wall of the third-floor conference room at the ODFW's headquarters in Salem, Oregon. Every box is bulging at the sides with reams of notes collected from 2003 to 2005, when the planning process for the Oregon Wolf Plan (OWP) was underway. One-third of the boxes are filled with public comments. The letters are scrawled in shaky cursive and block lettering, typed on business letterhead in Times New Roman, and signed by construction company presidents, retired professors of animal science, the president of the Oregon Farm Bureau, the secretary of Backcountry Hunters and Anglers, and thousands upon thousands of regular Oregonians, including the entirety of Mr. Bailey's fourth-grade class from Hazeldale Elementary School in Aloha, Oregon. These letters are bundled together with a paper clip the size of my thumb. The following is an excerpt from the top of the pile (reprinted verbatim):

> Dear ODFW: In my opinion, we, the Oregonians, should accept wolves into our state. Wolves will balance our ecosystem if we give them the chance. I understand the issue with wolves killing livestock. I find it appropriate to kill a wolf if that wolf is caught consuming a ranchers' livestock . . . If we work hard, the wolf can roam freely in Oregon again. Sincerely, Alec E. Age 10.

Another submission, this one left on an ODFW comment sheet and titled "What do you think about Wolves in Oregon," shows a hand-sketched wolf underneath a circle with a slash through it—a universal sign for No Wolves that is repeated by the phrase "Lobos Nada" printed in all caps at the bottom of the page. A note in the upper corner says it was sent in from Baker City, Oregon.

I spend hours leafing through the comments, but I could spend weeks. I spread them out on the table and the floor and move wobbly stacks of paper from one pile to another in an attempt to impose order. The voices behind the comments rise off the page and divide into two largely straightforward camps: "Yes, we want wolves," or "No, wolves should not be allowed in the state." Eventually, time and the repetitive nature of the notes prompt me to move on to the fourteen waiting boxes that contain the details and minutes from the actual WAC meetings, which served to create the state's wolf management plan.

The first meeting of the newly formed WAC was held the week before Thanksgiving in November 2003 at the Silver Falls State Park conference center outside Silverton, Oregon. A few memorable things happened. The first was that despite the low elevation of the park it snowed several inches— enough that travel became difficult and the conference center took on an isolated feeling. It felt like the group had been sequestered in the middle of the woods, said De Morgan. A lot of things could have happened out there that no one would have ever found out about. "I remember thinking the storm was either a sign of good things to come, or a signal of bad tidings," said De Morgan, who talked to me over the phone from his home in Utah while I sifted through the WAC documents. "Then because of how the center is organized, some of the committee members ended up having to share rooms. Many of them had never met, most disagreed on at least a few issues, and here they were being asked to share at least a bathroom and in some cases a bedroom, as well."

The movie adaptation of Stephen King's *The Shining* starring Jack Nicholson wielding a bloody red axe comes to mind, but De Morgan's notes assure that all WAC members survived the meeting, though there were some bumps and bruises that began with the introductions. The fourteen group members were asked to provide a brief personal background and their reasoning behind their decision to participate in the planning process.

Meg Mitchell had worked for the US Forest Service for sixteen years, ten of which were in Alaska, where she regularly worked with the issues specific to large predator and habitat management. She had previous experience and specialized knowledge of natural resource conflict resolution, collaboration, and public involvement. In addition, she was a ranger on the 2.2-million-acre Wallowa-Whitman National Forest in northeastern Oregon, where wolves were anticipated to first enter the state. Mitchell represented public lands managers.

Hans Radtke had worked in the fields of economics and natural resource use for more than thirty years. He served as chairman of the Pacific Fishery Management Council on the Oregon coast and believed the economic considerations of natural resource management should take into account all Oregonians, whether they were directly or indirectly related to the issues. Radtke represented economists.

Dan Edge had more than eighteen years of experience as an internationally recognized educator and wildlife scientist. He was head of the Department of Fish and Wildlife at Oregon State University and had served as the extension wildlife specialist for the state for ten years. He had held elected offices with The Wildlife Society at state, national, and international levels. When asked whether his statements and solutions would be acceptable to other members of the WAC, he replied, "Maybe." Edge represented educators.

Bill Gawloski was a retired grocery store manager and had managed stores for Safeway for ten years. He had a bachelor's degree in marketing and had lived in Silverton for thirty-one years. In his nomination letter to the state Fish and Wildlife Commission he wrote, "Myths and misconceptions sometimes cloud the true nature of the animals, and their impact on the people and animals must be clearly understood by all parties involved." Gawloski represented citizens-at-large from the west side of the state.

Joe Colver had been a commercial trapper for more than thirty years. He was the organizer of the Oregon Trapper's Association and represented the trapping community to ODFW. He had been part of several committees and groups involved in the creation and modification of some of Oregon's trapping and hunting laws. Colver represented trappers.

Amaroq Weiss was the western director of species conservation for Defenders of Wildlife. In 1997, she gave up a job as a lawyer with the Federal Defenders of San Diego to pursue a career related to wolf issues. Weiss was special projects leader at the California Wolf Center for three years. There she focused on public education. Weiss represented wolf conservationists.

Clint Krebs was the owner and manager of Krebs Ranches—a family operation that ran livestock in Wallowa, Morrow, and Gilliam Counties. He was a former president of the Oregon Sheep Growers Association and had sat on the boards of Oregon Country Beef, the National Lamb Feeders Association, and the Oregon Sheep Commission. In his nomination to the commission Krebs wrote, "I have an interest in protecting the natural ecosystem and balancing the rights of landowners to use the property they own to make a living." Krebs represented rural Oregon residents.

Ken Hall worked for the tribal Department of Natural Resources in fish and wildlife conservation and restoration. He was a past chair of the Confederated Tribes of the Umatilla Indian Reservation Tribal Board of Trustees, and a founding board member of the Umatilla Basin Watershed Council. Hall represented Native American tribes.

Sharon Beck was a fourth-generation rancher in Oregon. She was the past president of the Oregon Cattlemen's Association (OCA) and served four appointments as chair of the OCA's wolf task force. Beck had led the National Cattlemen's Beef Association's Endangered Species Committee and had been involved in several state and federal lawsuits related to land and species management. In 1999, Oregon representative Greg Walden paid formal tribute to Beck, saying, "She is a woman who has devoted a significant portion of her life to defending the farmers and ranchers of both Oregon and the United States and preserving their rural way of life." Beck represented livestock producers.

Ben Boswell was a Wallowa County commissioner who had been involved in wolf issues since his term began in 1993. As part of the Board of Commissioners he had helped pass an ordinance "prohibiting the reintroduction of any native species without the concurrence of the county governing body." Boswell had organized the 2000 Wallowa County Wolf Summit and had been heavily involved in delivering comments and testimony to the state legislature about the potential impact of wolves in Wallowa County, and about wolves as predators. He represented eastern Oregon county commissioners.

Sandy Sanderson had spent eleven years as chapter president of the Oregon Hunters Association. He was an active member of Ducks Unlimited and the Rocky Mountain Elk Foundation and had assisted the ODFW in the formulation of the state's Elk Management Plan. In his nomination letter to the commission, Sanderson wrote, "I believe when the wolf comes to Oregon, a plan should be in place to manage them as we have done with bear and cougar. We must keep science in the forefront and emotions on the back burner." He represented hunters.

Brett Brownscombe was the conservation director of the Hells Canyon Preservation Council. He led various state wildland and forest advocacy groups in their work related to wolf advocacy. In its nomination letter to the commission, the Oregon Natural Resources Council wrote, "Without Brett, the Advisory Committee would lack any credibility at all. He has spent many years of his life—including both professional and personal time—studying and working on wolf issues." Brownscombe represented range and forestland conservationists.

Robert Lund was a livestock investigator of the Oregon Department of Agriculture and a board member of the Oregon Hunters Association. A former Oregon State Police officer, he was part of the state's fish and wildlife regulatory division. Lund represented citizens-at-large from the east side of the state.

Robert Riggs was a wildlife researcher from the private sector. He had served on the Rocky Mountain Elk Foundation's Oregon Project Advisory Committee, the Western Wildlife Technical Committee for the National Council for Air and Stream Improvement, and the Ungulate Expert Panel for the Interior Columbia River Basin Ecosystem Assessment. Riggs represented wildlife biologists and researchers.

Also in attendance were a handful of audience members, ODFW northeastern office staff Mark Henjum and Craig Ely, and state Fish and Wildlife Commission chair Marla Rae.

"Going around the room that first night the majority of people seemed willing to listen to one another and we were respectful of other viewpoints," said Edge, who had to leave the committee midway through the process when he was appointed chair of the state Fish and Wildlife Commission. "But there were a few individuals who started off on the defensive. They were there to represent their viewpoint only and from the get-go they were looking for a fight."

Once everyone was introduced, De Morgan stood before the group, and much like a second-grade teacher on the first day of school, he laid down some ground rules:

• Focus on the task at hand.
• One person speaks at a time.
• Allow for a balance of speaking time. Everyone gets a turn.
• Be nice: No personal attacks. Be tough on the issues and questions, not on each other or the organizations they represent. Be a respectful listener. Keep side conversations to a minimum.
• Turn off cell phones or put them in nonring mode during formal meeting sessions.

These were grown men and women, professionals in their fields, but De Morgan repeated to them that following these rules would not always be easy, and that while it was his job to enforce good behavior, he would need their assistance in holding each other, themselves, and the group accountable. The WAC agreed to try. Then De Morgan gave Commission Chair Rae the floor.

Rae was a fifth-generation Oregonian, born on the east side of the state but raised in the Willamette Valley. Her appointment to chair was largely well received throughout the state. In a welcoming tone, Rae thanked the group for its time and commitment to the process. Then, while seeming to weigh the mettle of the individuals around the table, she continued.

"This process is designed to result in a predetermined course of action to follow when, as the experts say, wolves come to Oregon," she said, adding that the commission had selected each person on the committee because when combined into a group, they represented the most balanced set of interests possible. It is not the role of the committee to "put the pen to paper," she said. Rather, it is the committee's job to advise ODFW staff in the initial writing of the plan. She reminded the WAC that the commission would retain final decision-making authority for the plan. She then reiterated that the WAC was to focus on how to manage wolves in Oregon, not whether they should be allowed in the state in the first place.

This was key to structuring how the months ahead would unfold, said De Morgan. Over and over in Rae's opening remarks she thanked the committee for their commitment to the process and then reminded them that their job was to figure out the "how" of management. "They were told very specifically to come back with a plan that could be implemented when wolves arrived in the state," he said.

The WAC broke into discussion, and some of De Morgan's ground rules were immediately tested. However, out of the conversation came a few points that later became key to the overall plan. In brief, these points were as follows: The WAC was to learn from other states' wolf plans and not attempt to reinvent the wheel; Oregon's plan had to be consistent with laws for management dictated by the state's Endangered Species Act (ESA); only scenarios using the current status of wolves under the state and federal ESAs would be considered; the plan must accept and account for the natural dispersal of wolves from neighboring states; despite public lands making up a significant component of the area in northeastern Oregon and being used extensively by both ranchers and wildlife, the management of these lands would not fall within the authority of the WAC or the plan.

Again, the WAC erupted. This time the edge was a bit sharper as individuals shared their concerns and expectations related to the wide variety of opinions at the table, the presumed willingness of individuals to learn from one another, the necessity for sound scientific research, and the fact that the success of the plan could be judged only well into the future.

The meeting wound down with a presentation from the ODFW staff about recent wolf activity in the state and a review of the planning process, including an introduction to the plan's framework. The assistant attorney general for the Natural Resources Section of the Oregon Department of Justice then described both the legal guidelines for which the committee was responsible and the details of the wolf's current legal protection status both federally and in the state.

"At that point with the exception of a few people, everyone was in pretty good spirits as it related to the process," said De Morgan. The committee confirmed its next meeting, which was to be held January 12–13 in La Grande, Oregon, and then adjourned.

Making the Plan

The La Grande meeting passed largely without incident. The WAC reviewed its operation guidelines and then received briefings on wolf biology and ecology, the temporary federal strategy for managing wolves in Oregon, and historical wolf issues in the state. Committee members adopted a goal statement and planned a meeting schedule for the coming months. It was decided the committee would meet at various locations around the state both to lessen the travel burden on any individual member and to provide a greater view of the landscape in which wolves would be managed.

It wasn't until the WAC's February meeting that the novelty and shine of the process really began to show signs of wear. The meeting, held at the ODFW office in Salem, Oregon, focused on species conservation, budget implementation, and preparation for the next two meetings, which would concentrate on the interaction of wolves with other species. Once talks about conservation began, emotions started to get stirred up pretty quickly, said Craig Ely, who in his role as the northeast's regional manager for the ODFW was required to attend all the meetings. "As we moved further into the process, the members became more and more strident in their stances. By the third meeting their politics were showing."

It became apparent that there had been a fair amount of lobbying and maneuvering behind the nomination process for the committee, said Ely.

There were several agendas at the table, and not many remained hidden once a few months had passed.[1] It was clear that some of the nominations—the basis upon which committee members had been selected—had contained platitudes, and upon testing there were a fair number of statements and promises that proved disingenuous, said Ely.

Despite the state commission's guidelines that the WAC was not to debate whether wolves should be in the state, the issue kept coming up in conversation. Repeatedly the interests of eastern Oregon counties and cattle ranchers were said to be incompatible with wolves in areas where ranching occurred. The question of why wolves should be welcomed into the region now when the area had done fine without them for more than fifty years was repeatedly asked, and it was suggested that wolves would be the downfall of family ranchers in the state.

At the close of the third meeting, Henjum, the ODFW employee who was responsible for actually "putting the pen to paper" and drafting the plan, alerted the group that the next section of the plan to be addressed would relate to wolf interactions with domestic animals and with humans. While all aspects of the plan were important, these were especially hot-button issues, said Henjum. Committee members agreed that prior to the next meeting, in March, they would submit written comments providing insight into their individual interests and potential issues of which other members may not have been aware. "There was substantial tension in the room," said Henjum, who now works for the US Forest Service in Oregon's Umatilla Ranger District. "It was clear that there was going to be some conflict, but we needed to be able to find a reasonable and credible middle ground that would meet the needs of stakeholders and the regulating laws."

Fear about what wolves eat and how they hunt was the primary reason behind the extirpation of wolves in the early 1900s. Interactions between wolves and other species, especially prey species, continued to be a primary source of concern voiced by the general public during the fourteen town hall meetings held by the ODFW prior to beginning the formal planning process. It would not be an overstatement to say the management of these interactions would be the predominant factor in the overall success or failure of the conservation and management plan. Given that, it was surprising that only seven of the fourteen committee members submitted their thoughts on the topic prior to the March meeting. Notably absent were comments from representatives of cattle and ranching interests, the eastern Oregon counties, and the wildlife biologists.

Comments were received from those representing conservation, education, hunters, the public, and the economy. These fell largely into requests for more information, especially regarding numbers of livestock lost to wolves in states with established populations; discussions related to the responsibility of livestock owners to protect their animals; conflict response should depredation of domestic livestock occur; the translocation of packs in areas with high potential for conflict; and the need for an increased focus on public education and outreach. The submitted comments were shared with fourteen members of the WAC for discussion at the fourth meeting, held in Bend, Oregon. It didn't take long for a firestorm to break out.

On one side of the table, members seemed to believe that wolves would come onto the landscape, decimate elk and deer populations, kill domestic livestock for sport, and destroy the livelihood of Oregon's ranching families. On the other side, members agreed that there would be livestock and wildlife lost to wolves, but those losses would likely fall into acceptable levels and could be mitigated by proper management and responsible animal husbandry practices. In addition, wolves would add to the overall ecological diversity of the state and could result in overall increases in wildlife populations. The conversation ping-ponged back and forth. There were issues over terms like "responsible management" and "acceptable levels." Acceptable to whom? Faces grew red and tempers flared, but progress was made, said facilitator De Morgan.

There was a definite pattern to the process. A section of the plan would be introduced and presented to the group, with an explanation of any technical aspects. Then the members would discuss the topic and defend their positions, often adamantly. "As the meetings wore on small factions formed within the group," said Henjum, who describes the meetings as almost cliquish. "After a point there were representatives from both sides who refused to budge from their positions, but there were also some very reasoned people. It was a long process with a lot of bends and curves."

Throughout the spring and into the summer the WAC continued to meet. Committee members traveled to Medford, Pendleton, and back to Salem. At the June meeting, the first full draft of the plan was delivered to committee members for their review. With it came the reminder that according to the ODFW and in agreement with the US Fish and Wildlife Service and the US Department of Agriculture's Wildlife Services, the sole purpose of the plan was to "prepare for a coordinated and effective response to possible situations that may arise as gray wolves move, under their own power, into Oregon from adjacent states."

The resistance and opposition to large parts of the initial plan were substantial, said Henjum. Even after more than seven months, in some cases the entire foundation of the plan was called into question. "There were fourteen sets of eyes combing through every word," said Henjum, adding that some members were looking specifically for items in the draft with which to disagree. "It was necessary to develop a thick skin."

The committee was asked to read through the plan noting and commenting on areas of concern. They then gave their notes to De Morgan and the ODFW staff to compile into a matrix that divided the plan by chapters and sections. The WAC's comments were separated into two categories: category A, major substantive comments; and category B, minor substantive and major editorial; and these were fed into the matrix.

Category A contained thirty-five comments. Beck, representing livestock producers, wrote ten of them; Krebs, Brownscombe, and Weiss wrote seven apiece; Sanderson put in three; and Bret Michalski, who had replaced Edge as the educators' representative, submitted one comment. Category B garnered another nineteen comments, with Riggs, Weiss, Beck, Radtke, and Brownscombe all citing at least one area of concern.

The WAC spent the next two months revising and going over the plan, often line by line, in an attempt to resolve the concerns raised by the committee members. Its original goal was to reach a unanimous consensus before sending the plan to the Fish and Wildlife Commission at the beginning of September. However, it became clear that a majority might be the best they could do. "I was hopeful we would get nine or ten of the committee members to sign on to the plan," said Ely, who added that at the last review nearly half of the WAC still had major concerns with at least a portion of the plan. "I was ecstatic when we got twelve of the fourteen."

Boswell and Beck were the dissidents. In his official minority report, Boswell wrote, "I remain convinced that an effort to establish wolves in Oregon is a fool's errand. Having received a crash course in wolf ecology over the past year, I have concluded that lots of wildlife will die, some livestock will die and many wolves will die. Why do we want to embark on a plan to permit this agent of death to populate our state? I believe we do not. I propose that wolves be kept from Oregon by whatever means necessary."

Beck also filed a minority report, stating, "This plan is unduly complicated and wordy. . . . It is sprinkled with inaccuracies that seem intended to bias the reader. The context of the plan implies that the wolf is a fragile species whose survival is always on the brink of extinction. The very fact that we cannot shoot it, trap it or poison it, virtually assures its vigorous survival and increase of potentially over 30% each year."

On September 9, 2004, the WAC presented the Oregon Wolf Conservation and Management Plan (OWP) to the state Fish and Wildlife Commission. The document called for a conservation approach to wolf management in the state, allowing for the establishment of wolves that migrate into Oregon through natural dispersal, and asked for human tolerance of the species. It divided the state into two management areas separated by the Cascade Range and assigned different population goals for each region. It allowed for the possibility of managers transferring wolves from the east side of the state to the west side in order to achieve the overall conservation goal of four breeding pairs of wolves present in each region for three consecutive years.

Also included in the plan were an outline for the establishment of management agreements with other agencies, like the USDA Wildlife Services; a strategy for implementing a comprehensive wolf monitoring program; and a call for the reclassification of wolves' legal status to a "special status game mammal" once wolves were removed from the state and federal Endangered Species Lists. The change in classification would allow for a more diverse management strategy in the future; one that could include hunting and trapping.

The WAC employed a three-phase implementation strategy within the plan. The first stage called for achieving population objectives set by the state and protecting wolves from lethal removal, except under special circumstances. Phase two focused on achieving the population objective of seven breeding pairs for three consecutive years. Phase three emphasized maintenance of the wolf population so that it would neither fall below phase one objectives nor grow to a point that would result in conflict with other land uses.

"The plan was created as a set of tools that opened a door so managers would know what to do when wolves arrived," said Henjum. "It was a living document that was designed for active use."

After the commission received and reviewed the draft plan, it was made public. ODFW employees spent much of the fall and early winter presenting the plan to communities and stakeholder groups around the state. After a month and a half, more than eight hundred public comments on the plan had been received. According to the ODFW, 39 percent supported the draft plan, 9 percent did not support it, 27 percent offered general comments about wolves, and 25 percent recommended changes to the draft plan. At the end of the three-month period allotted for public review, almost two thousand comments had been submitted to the state. "I'd never seen anything like it," said Henjum. "No one in the state had ever had any personal experience with this animal, yet there was so much emotion."

On February 11, 2005, the commission officially adopted Oregon's first Wolf Conservation and Management Plan. It faced immediate resistance, and revisions to the plan began at once.[2] Yet despite that, Oregon had succeeded in putting a committee-designed management plan in place. Now, it was just a matter of waiting for wolves to show up. It didn't take long.

Early Arrivals

It is the middle of July in a long, hot summer. The calendar says 2008. It has been three years since the wolf plan was signed, and the state has confirmed the presence of only one live wolf. B-300, a radio-collared female from an Idaho pack, was captured on video in January 2008 as she traveled in the Wallowa-Whitman National Forest near the Eagle Cap Wilderness outside Joseph, Oregon. Other wolves had been reported at various locations in the state, but without substantive evidence, the sightings were labeled as either "possible" or "hearsay" depending on who was giving the account. In addition, a wolf carcass was found in Union County in May 2007. The animal was badly decomposed, but forensic analysis established the wolf was a female related to the Idaho population and had been killed by a gunshot wound.

The lack of confirmed wolves in the state is gnawing at Russ Morgan, who has been on the job as Oregon's wolf coordinator for almost two years. He knows there are wolves out here, but like so many other people who believe there are wolves in their neighborhood, he doesn't have any proof. It's not for lack of trying. For the last eight months since observing possible wolf sign during elk hunting season, Morgan has regularly driven deep into a forested area in northern Union County, cupped his hands to his mouth, and let out long, loud AAWWOOOOooooos.

His howls are part of a bona fide scientific survey technique wildlife managers use to identify the presence of wolves in areas too large to survey visually. Territorial wolf packs and individual wolves will often respond and move toward the human howlers across distances of several miles. However, it's not a perfect tool. Wolves have been known to ignore or not respond to the howls of humans and other wolves. In addition, when a response is elicited it provides only general information about whether or not a wolf, or wolves, are present. Deducing more specific information about the exact size of the population and the sex and age of wolves within it can be a stretch.

Still, any response is better than no response, and howling surveys offer a practical, low-cost option for trying to determine whether wolves are in an area. That potential for success, no matter how slim, is why Morgan's voice is now hoarse enough to sand paint, and why he has spent the last two days eating peanut butter sandwiches and sleeping in the dirt next to the truck. Exhausted and staring blankly out the windshield, with sweat dripping from his forehead and mosquitoes buzzing around his ears, Morgan decides that one more night will have to be enough.

Driving down the washboarded fire road at fifteen miles per hour, Morgan can feel every bump and jolt in his kidneys. Dry summer dust comes in through the vents in the truck's dash and coats the interior with the same fine brown film covering the undergrowth and Douglas-fir trees at the roadside. Every ten minutes or so, Morgan stops, rolls down his window, and howls. He keeps it up for one hour, two hours, four. At about 1:00 a.m he pulls the truck to the shoulder, switches off the engine and, being too tired to even pull out his sleeping bag, lets his head loll back against the seat. He sleeps for almost two hours propped in the driver's seat. Waking at roughly 3:00 a.m., he decides it couldn't hurt to howl into the darkness. When a responding howl comes immediately and from less than twenty-five yards away, Morgan almost falls out of the cab. Before the howl ends it is joined by another, deeper howl that in turn is punctuated by higher-pitched yips—the sound of pups.

"They were right there probably the whole time I had been sleeping," said Morgan. "A whole family." Though he couldn't see the wolves, their voices provided proof that not only one wolf but a whole group, complete with multiple adults and pups, was in Oregon. The ensemble of howls was the first evidence of wolf reproduction occurring in the state in more than sixty years. Suddenly Morgan was no longer tired. He spent the next hour listening to the wolves as they retreated back into the forest.

In the morning, making his way down the drainage, Morgan stops a few more times to howl. He doesn't receive any response, but now he knows with certainty that wolves are out there in the Wenaha River drainage. Driving the eighty miles back to the ODFW field office in La Grande, he begins to think about the implementation of the OWP and how it will apply to the monitoring and tracking of the Wenaha wolves.

By the standards settled upon in the OWP, Morgan's audible observations of multiple howling wolves carried a much larger significance for wolf recovery than the sighting of B-300. According to the OWP, one lone wolf did not carry much promise in terms of building a sustainable population. However, two adult wolves with two pups that survived to December 31 of the year of their birth could signify a breeding pair, and the first conservation goal of the plan was to establish four breeding pairs on either side of Oregon's Cascades. The next goal was to have each of those pairs remain together, successfully reproducing and rearing pups, for three consecutive years. If that happened, the plan said state officials could consider delisting wolves from Oregon's Endangered Species List. Once seven breeding pairs proved successful in the state, protections on the wolves could be further reduced and a hunting season potentially opened.

If that sounds complicated, it's because the reality is even more severe. In studies of exploited wolf populations in North America, the annual mortality rate of adult wolves averaged 37 percent. For pups the rate was higher, with 40 to 60 percent of pups dying each year. Despite the proclivity of wolves to breed, their success is not a given.

Learning more about the wolves and keeping track of their movements, habits, and numbers is key to species recovery. Phase one of the plan calls for the use of radiotelemetric collars, like those the Idaho wolves wore, for monitoring establishing breeding pairs and packs. Information about pack distribution, mortality, dispersal, den locations, prey sources, winter use areas, and territory boundaries could all be derived from the collars and used by the state to better understand wolves and to implement other aspects of the plan. The immediate challenge facing Morgan was how to best capture and collar the Wenaha wolves.

Morgan grew up hunting and trapping in central Oregon in the rural area between Bend and Prineville. He shot his first deer with a gun when he was fifteen and shot his first elk while in college at Oregon State University studying wildlife science. He started archery hunting after graduating from OSU in 1986, and in 1999 he started making his own bowhunting tackle and materials. His office is filled with pictures from past hunts that have taken him all over the West and into Canada and Alaska.

Not long after we first met, Morgan told me there is nothing he would rather do than track a wild animal. He said he didn't even need to catch it. It was the pursuit, and putting together a story of where the animal had traveled and why, that he loved. He said successful trapping meant being able to place a trap so precisely that in the middle of the wilderness an animal could not help but step in the two-inch by two-inch trigger area that would leave it caught. Trapping took a combination of being very, very skilled and very, very lucky.

In cooperation with the USFWS and Umatilla National Forest, Morgan began trapping in the area where he had heard the Wenaha wolves. As bait he used commercially sold scents that came double-wrapped in plastic and still had the UPS man plugging his nose, and deer and elk bones with scraps of meat still on them that he had saved from his own hunts for this specific use. Banking on wolves' territorial nature and marking habits, Morgan also asked his Idaho associates to mail scat from wolves there, which he then set up along areas he believed the Wenaha wolves might travel. He worked at it for months. One night he found wolf tracks around the traps, and one trap was triggered, but no wolves were captured.

On November 29, 2008, due to the onset of cold weather and concern for animal welfare, Morgan removed all traps from the area. It had been four months since he'd heard the Wenaha wolves' first howl. He made plans to resume trapping in the spring and to continue monitoring efforts through the winter.

For the next two months, he received periodic reports of wolf sightings in the Wenaha drainage and other areas of northeastern Oregon. In February 2009, Morgan and ODFW staff spent twelve days conducting snow track surveys via snowmobile. They located two sets of tracks in the Imnaha drainage, where B-300 had been previously sighted. Evidence found with the tracks showed the presence of both male and female wolves. Additionally there were signs that the female was in heat and ready to breed. Signals from B-300's radio collar were not found, but it was possible the collar had malfunctioned and she was still in the area. In the Wenaha drainage, tracks of a male and female pair were also found with signs of estrus. There was no evidence of the pups Morgan had heard in July.

Four days of monitoring in March found new wolf tracks in the Keating Valley outside Baker City, Oregon. The tracks appeared to be two wolves traveling together, but there was no useful evidence for determining the sex of either animal. As spring approached, Morgan planned to explore the area further to determine the likelihood of a breeding pair establishing a home territory in the Keating Valley. It turned out he didn't have time.

In the second week of April 2009, on two separate evenings, wolves entered fenced enclosures on Curt and Anne Jacobs's ranch in the Keating Valley and killed twenty-four lambs. Then, on April 16, a calf at a neighboring ranch was also killed. Night images taken from a trail camera at one of the ranches clearly showed two wolves, their eyes glowing, standing over the carcasses of the livestock. Tracks at the Jacobs's ranch and the results from a necropsy on the calf clearly showed wolves were responsible. These were likely the same animals whose tracks Morgan had followed in March, and not part of either the Wenaha or Imnaha groups. The depredations were the first by wolves in Oregon since the 1940s. Morgan, the USFWS, the USDA Wildlife Services, and the Oregon State Police were called immediately.

Wildlife Services and the State Police went to work performing flyovers to look for the wolves. Morgan essentially moved onto the Jacobs's ranch and began assisting with the implementation of nonlethal control methods, as outlined by the OWP. These methods were part of the plan's strategy to resolve conflict between wolves and livestock, while allowing for the conservation of wolves. If depredation continued after all nonlethal strategies had been deployed, the state could then consider lethally removing depredating wolves.

Morgan went to work stringing lines of electrically conductive wire around the tops of the animal enclosures. Dangling like tinsel from the wire were closely spaced, bright strips of fabric that danced and snapped in the breeze like thousands of small wind socks. Fladry, as this setup is called, has incurred moderate success in deterring wolves from livestock in some areas and under some circumstances. To further dissuade wolves from entering onto the property, Morgan also organized the cleanup of exposed cattle carcasses. These bone piles, which, as might be expected, are desirable attractants for scavenging animals, are common on many ranches and are often the product of a lack of time and adequate disposal options for cattle that die from disease or other causes. Morgan spent time talking with other landowners in the area. He asked them to be vigilant and to contact him or the ODFW offices if they had problems with predators or observed something out of the norm.

Then, joined by a USFWS agent and Idaho-based Carter Niemeyer, who at the time had likely trapped more wolves than anyone else in the nation, Morgan began tracking the two Keating Valley wolves. The men's intent was to trap and collar both wolves so the animals could be regularly monitored and their locations tracked. By keeping close tabs on the wolves and having nonlethal control measures in place, Morgan hoped future depredation would be avoided.

It was nineteen days before the group caught one of the wolves; a one-year-old male weighing eighty-seven pounds. The wolf was sedated, fitted with a radio collar, given a physical that included taking a tissue sample for genetic analysis, and then released. A smaller wolf was also observed at the time of capture but was not caught. It appeared to be a young female.

After collaring the male wolf, Morgan was able to track the pair as they moved together, first out of the valley, then back toward the ranches where they had found easy prey. Because he knew where the wolves were coming from and the direction in which they were headed, Morgan was able to organize a team to drive the animals away from the ranches using aircraft hazing and nonlethal on-the-ground methods, including rubber bullets and beanbag projectiles. The wolves returned to the area for five days running but were driven off each day. On May 18, signals from the radio collar showed the male wolf moving back into upper-elevation forest habitat, and it was assumed the female was with him. A week and a half later both wolves were sighted within the Eagle Cap Wilderness, more than thirty miles from the Keating Valley.

Before leaving the valley, Morgan issued the affected landowners radio receivers. If the depredating wolves returned to the area the receivers would pick up transmissions from the male's collar and alert the ranchers of the wolves' proximity to their livestock through a series of beeps. Morgan also installed a radio-activated guard (RAG) box on one of the ranches. RAG boxes are the equivalent of a home alarm system. When a radio-collar signal is detected by the system, a loud alarm and flashing lights are activated. Like fladry, RAG boxes have been shown effective in deterring predators in some circumstances; however, habituation to the boxes can occur, rendering the system largely useless. According to the OWP, managers working with livestock producers, both preemptively and after depredation, should employ techniques that will have the highest likelihood of success and that are reasonable for each individual situation. Radio-collaring the male wolf was perhaps the most effective tool available to help prevent further livestock losses, said the ODFW. Along with alerting managers and area ranchers to possible threats to livestock, the collar provided an opportunity for the state to increase its knowledge of how wolves were using the landscape. With this information, decisions could be made about the daily management of livestock in order to best protect against depredation.

In total, Morgan and the team of state and federal agents working on the Keating Valley depredations spent more than a month in the area tracking wolves and helping the community bolster its management. When Morgan finally returned to his office, it was with the knowledge that his job had become much more complicated. There had been considerable uproar and attention surrounding the livestock loss in the Keating Valley, and the scrutiny of the OWP and Morgan was increasing daily. For many people, the depredations in Keating Valley proved that wolves were bloodthirsty monsters, and these people had little acceptance of the nonlethal measures. They wanted the wolves not just monitored but gone completely.

Compared to May, June passed relatively quietly. The ODFW received ten reports of wolves or wolf tracks from around the state. None were confirmed. Morgan's team spent three days surveying for wolves in the Imnaha drainage. They found tracks and scat in the same general areas where sightings were made during the winter, but howling surveys and additional tracking produced no wolf sightings. The ODFW also continued to monitor OR-1, the male wolf Morgan had captured after the Keating Valley depredations. The state performed five aerial flyovers to confirm OR-1 had established territory in the newly recognized Keating Unit, an area of about 233 square miles adjacent to the Eagle Cap Wilderness.

July came and OR-1 seemed to be staying in the forested areas of the unit away from human population. It appeared the preventive measures had been successful, and while continuing to monitor OR-1 by his radio collar, the ODFW also began to expand its efforts to locate other reported wolves. The agency received a report of wolf pups in the Imnaha drainage, and Morgan was able to follow up on the call immediately. The fast response resulted in the capture of B-300. She was indeed still alive, but the collar she had been fitted with in Idaho had stopped working. Morgan placed a new collar around her neck and renamed her OR-2. During a routine physical examination given at the time of her capture, Morgan was able to confirm that she had recently given birth to pups, and he made plans to return to the area before the end of summer to attempt a full count of the litter. Another report offered potential insight about OR-2's possible mate. A large black wolf had been sighted near where OR-2 was captured and within the same time frame. Morgan added trapping for this wolf to his To Do list, which also included continued surveys of the Wenaha drainage, where the wolves remained quiet and elusive.

By August it was becoming clear that wolves were repopulating the eastern corner of the state. With the level of movement being observed, it seemed likely that it would be only a matter of time before there was another incident between wolves and humans. That incident occurred on August 28, 2009. Again the Jacobs's ranch in Keating Valley was at the center of the upheaval. In a manner nearly identical to the April depredations, wolves had entered a pen on the ranch and killed three sheep and a pet goat. According to an ODFW report, a fourth lamb died from its injuries the next morning. Track sizes, depredation history, and wounds found on the sheep solidly implicated OR-1 and his female companion in the losses. The depredations brought the total number of domestic livestock animals killed by wolves in 2009 to twenty-nine.

After the encounter Curt Jacobs told the *Baker City Herald*, "We think it happened around 3:45 on Friday morning. That's when my dogs and my neighbors' dogs up and down the river were going nuts. We went down and found a dead white-faced lamb. Then we saw the big wolf tracks in the mud. The ground was still wet from the storm."

Morgan and a host of other local, state, and federal officials again convened at the ranch. After taking stock of the situation and reviewing the measures they had gone through in the spring, the ODFW held OR-1 and his female companion responsible for the Keating Valley depredations. The state authorized Wildlife Services to lethally remove the wolves.

Prior to the establishment of seven successful breeding pairs in the state, the OWP allows for the lethal removal of wolves in only two very specific situations related to conflict with livestock. The first is a mechanism to stop a wolf in the act of attacking livestock, as defined by actively biting, wounding, or killing an animal. Lethal removal in this situation requires a government-approved permit, which will be issued only after the ODFW has confirmed that wolves have previously wounded or killed animals in the area and that all reasonable means to deter them have been tried and failed. The second is to stop wolves responsible for the chronic depredation of livestock. In these cases, state or federal agents will authorize lethal removal at a livestock owner's request if the state has previously confirmed two depredations in the area by wolves on livestock, or one confirmed depredation followed by three attempted depredations, and only if all nonlethal measures to prevent depredation have been implemented without success. Only authorized personnel will be allowed to perform the removal. "After all the nonlethal options have been explored and proven unsuccessful, the plan says lethal removal becomes an alternative, and chronic depredation of livestock is not something the state can tolerate," said Craig Ely, who retired from the ODFW in 2011. "Nobody wants to raise something to be killed."

Agents operating at the request of the state killed the wolves responsible for the Keating Valley depredations on September 5, 2009. While there was some backlash from the conservation community, there was general agreement that the wolves had become a problem and all reasonable options to deter them from killing livestock had been exhausted.

Throughout August and September 2009 the ODFW received thirty-four reports of wolves or tracks from the public. Most of the reports were confirmed as not being wolf. However, a few proved accurate, reinforcing the idea that wolves were entering Oregon, establishing new territories, and in some cases reproducing.

Depredation

It's just after noon on the last day of August 2012. On the phone Karl Patton's voice keeps getting louder. He's spitting his words, and they come through the receiver like verbal battering rams. I turn down the volume and hold the speaker a few inches from my ear. He abruptly stops talking, and I hear him take a deep breath that is almost a sigh. "I'm sorry," said Patton, who's been running cattle in Wallowa County since 1972. "It's just been incredibly frustrating."

Before calling me, Patton had come in for lunch and spent twenty minutes on the phone with Morgan at the ODFW. Patton had 150 pairs of calves out on Starvation Ridge above Swamp Creek in the Wallowa-Whitman National Forest, and he had heard through several people that wolves had been confirmed in the area the day before. He had called Morgan in an effort to find out if his cows were in danger and to ask about the existence and whereabouts of the rumored new pack of wolves. Morgan was able to confirm that two weeks earlier, the ODFW had spotted a black wolf in the Sled Springs management unit, an area that includes Swamp Creek and is defined by the Grande Ronde River on the west, Joseph Creek on the east, the Washington border on the north, and State Highway 82 on the south. This had been the second confirmed wolf sighting in the area, but because the ODFW had yet to capture and collar a wolf in the vicinity, Morgan could not tell Patton whether his animals were in any real danger.

As for the stories of another pack? Those were true. But the pack, which comprised two adults and five pups, was discovered in the Upper Minam River drainage. The Minam Unit borders the Sled Springs Unit to the southwest, and though the home range of the newly discovered wolves was not yet known, Patton said Morgan seemed to think it was unlikely the animals were traversing into the Swamp Creek area. "He couldn't say for certain where the wolves were hunting, only what he thought," said Patton of Morgan's response. "I spend so much time out here running in circles; I go from one place to another trying to find out accurate information. Then when I think I have it figured out I find out what I thought was true isn't. And all that time when my cows are out there, the wolves might be out there, too. There's so much wasted time."

Since the Keating Valley depredations almost three years ago, the ODFW has investigated and made reports on more than fifty-five incidents of livestock loss. From those investigations, the department confirmed that wolves have killed an additional twenty-nine domestic livestock animals. Ten of the animals lost were sheep killed in three incidents on ranches in Umatilla County. The remaining nineteen attacks were on cattle in Wallowa County in areas where members of the Imnaha pack had been sighted. Two of the attacks, occurring in February 2011, were on pregnant cows belonging to Patton.

The cows were killed on Patton's land in the Upper Wallowa Valley just outside of Joseph, Oregon. Patton found the animals in the morning and immediately called agents from the USDA Wildlife Services, the USFWS, and the ODFW. He also called Wallowa county sheriff Fred Steen, and Rod Childers, a neighbor and the chair of the Oregon Cattlemen's Association's (OCA) Wolf Task Force. In what had become a rare occurrence during previous investigations, all parties reached the same conclusion, that wolves were responsible for the depredations; however, the number and specific wolves involved was unresolved.

"That's four animals I've lost to wolves, and that's without counting all the animals that have gone missing," said Patton, who counts the unborn calves as losses. "If ODFW can't confirm a wolf kill then it doesn't count."

Having dead or missing animals confirmed as wolf kills by the ODFW is of paramount importance for Oregon ranchers. According to the OWP, verification of depredation by wolves carries consequences that can include a commitment by the ODFW to help prevent future depredations; monetary compensation up to the value of the animal killed, usually an amount between $800 and $1,500; and the potential for lethal control if the depredation is deemed chronic.

Because of these high-stakes consequences, the ODFW has a strict protocol for investigating possible depredations and confirming whether wolves have been involved. Often local officials and other agency representatives will perform their own investigations into livestock loss, and frequently the ODFW's conclusions have differed from other presented conclusions. In these cases the OWP states that the final decision lies with ODFW wildlife managers, and these discrepancies in findings are frequently made known to the public and to the impacted livestock producers. It's a situation that has done little to benefit relationships between the livestock community and the state agencies, said Morgan.

"When it comes to wolves, perception is everything, and there is often enormous emotion involved," said Morgan, adding that it can be very hard to be objective in an investigation when there is a dead calf lying in the dirt and an obviously upset rancher standing in the background. "Regardless of what people may think of my approach, my job is to follow, and implement, the state wolf plan."

When agency personnel are confronted with a dead cow, the first step in the OWP strategy for managing depredation is to determine whether or not the animal was actually killed by a wolf. That's not necessarily an easy thing to do. The ODFW uses a four-tiered classification system adopted from USDA Wildlife Services to assess the involvement of wolves in livestock injuries and mortality. The system is meant to encourage consistency across agencies, and its categories are other, possible/unknown, probable, and confirmed. It's similar to the spiciness ratings for salsa. There's mild, medium, hot, and melt your face off, and there's no doubt it's the last one that means business.

In order for the ODFW to confirm a depredation as being caused by a wolf, two criteria must be met: (1) there must be physical evidence that the animal was attacked and/or killed by a predator, and (2) if the first criterion is met, there must be evidence that the predator was a wolf. If these criteria are not met, agents cannot confirm wolves were responsible for the livestock loss. Instead they must make a classification that allows for the possibility that an accident, disease, or nonwolf predator led to the incident.

There are a variety of predators in Oregon that prey on domestic livestock. Coyotes, black bears, and cougars regularly kill cattle and sheep in all parts of the state. Coyotes are responsible for the majority of livestock depredation, and a USDA Wildlife Services report on the number of animals lost to predators states that the small canids killed an average of 222 cows and 1,408 sheep in Oregon each year between 1996 and 2002. Disease, parasites, accidents, and a range of other maladies also regularly result in the deaths of livestock. That's not to let wolves off the hook, but it is important to recognize that there are many factors involved in livestock loss.

"We've always had predators," agreed Patton. "Several years ago we had a mama cat down in the lower Imnaha and she was teaching her kittens how to kill cows. We lost several animals. The difference was that we knew she was down there and we could call some guys with hounds to go take care of her. We didn't have to sit and watch our animals disappear, or call for an investigation that might not result in anything. We could do something."

Therein lies the rub for Patton and many of Oregon's ranchers living in areas being repopulated by wolves. Because wolves are protected under the state's Endangered Species Act, it is a criminal offense punishable by fines and jail time for a member of the public to harm, or contribute to the harm of, a wolf in Oregon.[1] All decisions related to wolves in the state fall to the ODFW, and the agency is required to manage in accordance with the OWP.[2] "There are a lot of people here who talk about the shoot, shovel, and shut up style of management, and how that's the best option for managing these wolves," said Patton. "But if you do anything and you get caught you're going to prison. I don't know many guys willing to take that risk."

In the case of depredations, the OWP specifically states that livestock owners cannot take lethal action against wolves unless they have been granted a permit by the state and unless they catch the wolves actively attacking their animals. In addition, livestock owners are not allowed to partake in potentially injurious harassment activities, including the use of rubber bullets or pursuit-oriented hazing of wolves on their property, without a permit. They are, however, given a host of nonlethal, noninjurious methods to preemptively protect their animals from attack. These methods must be employed before any other action, including the granting of permits, is considered by the state.

The 2011 depredations on Patton's property resulted in a cooperative project between a Wallowa County community organization and the USFWS to install fladry around Patton's calving pastures and the pastures of several other livestock owners in the vicinity. The ODFW also placed a RAG box, similar to the alarm-like box used at the Jacobs's ranch in Keating Valley, on Patton's land to deter collared wolves from entering the area. Though supportive of these efforts on his land, Patton said he isn't sure the nonlethal preventive measures make sense for cattle ranchers. He doubts their efficacy and said that in the case of fladry, the frequent moving of cows to different areas for forage and disease prevention is prohibitive to stringing the fencing. He's not alone in his doubts.

Some of the nation's preeminent researchers have called into question the ability of nonlethal control measures, including fladry and RAG boxes, to stop wolves from preying on domestic livestock. David Mech said that short of eradicating wolves in areas near livestock, humans have not yet been able to find a way to stop depredation over the long term.[3] Livestock conflict is the primary problem facing wolf conservation today, but very few people who have a stake in the game are willing to admit to it.

When I asked Morgan if nonlethal control measures worked to prevent depredation, he hedged. So did Dan Edge, who sat on the Wolf Advisory Committee and has spent years as an internationally recognized wildlife researcher. Carter Niemeyer, who probably has more on-the-ground experience trapping wolves in the West than anyone, hemmed and hawed. Sometimes, and in some cases, but only if depredation isn't chronic, was the best answer I could get from any of them.

Mech wrote that wolves prey on livestock wherever they coexist. However, he knew of no place in North America where livestock were the primary source of prey for wolves, or where wolves relied on livestock for survival.[4] That provides a bit of hope for protecting livestock in northeastern Oregon, where wild prey is plentiful. However, the overall ineffectiveness associated with nonlethal control methods for depredating wolves is a bitter pill to swallow for many people and organizations wanting to see wolves and humans sharing the landscape in harmony.

In an effort to bolster available methods of nonlethal predator control, Defenders of Wildlife, a national nonprofit organization that has been heavily involved in wolf conservation, wrote a manual titled *Livestock and Wolves: A Guide to Nonlethal Tools and Methods to Reduce Conflicts*. The group invited a range of stakeholders to provide suggestions and content for the manual. Amaroq Weiss, who was also part of Oregon's Wolf Advisory Committee, was part of the editorial team involved in creating the guide. Defenders suggested that before implementing any strategy for nonlethal protection, livestock owners consider the number, age, and type of livestock needing protection; the season in which animals would be vulnerable; the location, accessibility, and size of the grazing area; and how often the animals would be under human supervision.

Many of the strategies that might work for small sheep operations are going to be ineffective for cattle ranchers running hundreds of head. In addition, experience has shown that livestock depredation by wolves in Oregon happens most frequently in the spring and early summer, when pups are born, and in the fall, when it is assumed the animals are trying to put on weight prior to winter. Ranchers in Oregon and much of the West have received extensive criticism for their management practices once their animals are released onto summer grazing allotments on public lands. While public lands use is a contentious issue in its own right, it is worth noting that up until 2012, all confirmed livestock depredations in Oregon occurred on private lands, often within a relatively short distance of homes and communities.

According to the Defenders guide, specific preventive strategies for wolf depredation include the reduction of attractants like bone piles and the afterbirth from calving; the use of specially trained livestock-guarding dogs; permanent, portable, and temporary fencing that may or may not use fladry; an increase in human presence through the employment of range riders and herders; and the incorporation of scare tools and tactics like RAG boxes, shock collars similar to those used in some types of dog training, and nonlethal ammunition. If these measures fail, Defenders suggests that livestock producers consider switching grazing sites, raising different breeds of animals that may be more capable of resisting predator attacks, or changing the time of year calving season occurs through shifts in breeding dates.

Several of these ideas seem like common sense. Burying dead animals and cleaning up after calving are easy examples, and they seem like practices everyone can, and should, follow. But it's worth remembering that many livestock producers have spent the majority of their careers not having to think about wolves. Some things that might seem like obvious attractants to predators have been standard practice for more than fifty years. Regardless, in the big scheme of things, these are doable changes. Even installing fencing and training guard dogs for use during calving season are straightforward, and in many cases reasonable, approaches to livestock management. It's the practices further down the list that seem to raise problems and eyebrows in Oregon.

Breeding different types of cattle, finding new grazing areas, or changing calving schedules and techniques often require fundamental transformations by livestock producers—transformations that may demand large amounts of investment, and often some degree of risk. Economically, these types of changes are out of reach for many of Oregon's ranchers who struggle to maintain the status quo. "There are a lot of people out there saying they want wolves in Oregon regardless of the consequences," said Patton. "What I want is to keep running cattle. I've been on ranches since 1972. I started in high school, and it's the only thing I've ever done or wanted to do. How does that fit with them wanting wolves?"

After Patton's two pregnant cows were killed, Rod Childers of the OCA said that the animals had been ripped open, the fetuses dragged across the ground, the soft tissue devoured, and the bones gnawed. Speaking on behalf of the cattlemen's group, Childers told the state's agricultural newspaper that the depredations at Patton's were the last straw and the OCA would be requesting the lethal removal of the wolves, in part because of the level of violence involved.

While the depredations were indeed ugly, the gory dismantling of the carcasses was not due to an evil streak in the wolves. With all large prey, wolves usually first open the body cavity using their teeth and claws. They then pull out and consume the larger internal organs (heart, lungs, and liver), which are nutritionally dense. They then eat the stomach lining and intestinal wall before moving on to the smaller organs.[5] After consuming the vital organs, wolves will move on to the large muscle groups and will often eat until their stomachs are engorged with meat. They then leave the prey site and head into the hills to sleep and digest.

While not typical in that most attacks on cattle usually involve only a single animal being killed or wounded,[6] the incident with Patton's two cows did highlight a few important characteristics of cattle depredations. First, few attacks on cattle are ever actually witnessed. Most attacks occur at night, and carcasses are not usually discovered until hours after predation has occurred. Second, without detailed genetic analysis it is rarely possible to identify specific wolves involved in depredations. This has important ramifications if or when wolves are targeted for lethal removal. Finally, it is widely acknowledged that wolves kill more domestic animals grazing in heavily forested areas with minimal management then they do on cleared, intensively managed pastureland. Yet this does not mean wolves will not approach human settlements or cross open pasture in pursuit of prey. The truth is that when compared with running down an elk in a rugged wilderness, killing domestic livestock in smooth pasturelands without deterrents may provide wolves an easy high-calorie meal. In these scenarios, undefended ranches can become the McDonald's drive-through of the predator set. It's a matter of convenience, and as stated by Mech, in the majority of cases wolves do not need to eat livestock to survive.

In healthy ecosystems, wolves are more than capable of surviving on wild prey. Able to travel upward of forty miles in a day and capable of reaching top speeds of thirty-four to thirty-eight miles per hour, wolves are well adapted to covering vast stretches of land in pursuit of a meal. A fair amount of wild prey is located through chance encounters that occur while traveling (on average, 30 percent of a wolf's time spent traveling doubles as hunting time).[7] However, wolves also use their keen senses to find and track prey. Their hunting strategy often incorporates careful stalking of prey followed by a quick chase. If the prey animals hold their ground or approach the wolves, the wolves will usually abandon the hunt.[8] Only about 8 percent of all hunts result in prey mortality and a full belly for the wolves. So while wolves do not need livestock, the attraction is apparent.

Ten days after the depredations on Patton's cows, the ODFW captured two yearling wolves from the Imnaha pack. Working with a team of wildlife biologists from the USFWS and the Wallowa-Whitman National Forest, Morgan conducted physicals and genetic sampling on the sedated male and female and fit both animals with GPS collars, an upgrade from the radio collars that he had been using on previously captured wolves.[9] A day later, the team captured and collared a third Imnaha wolf, a two-year-old male. The captures were made possible by following the radio collars worn by OR-2, the pack's alpha female, and another collared adult in the pack. The team also attempted to capture the pack's alpha male but was unsuccessful. The alpha male had previously been captured and collared, but his collar had stopped working after only a few months.

A few months later, the Imnaha pack was implicated in two fatal attacks on cattle; one was confirmed as a wolf depredation, and the other was classified as probable by the ODFW in collaboration with the USFWS. The outrage from area ranchers was palpable, and Childers once again stepped in to speak for cattlemen, requesting that the Imnaha wolves be lethally removed. While some of the state and federal agents may have been willing to consider the request, a series of unresolved political and legal situations related to the delisting and relisting of wolves to the federal Endangered Species List and the transfer of management back and forth between the ODFW and the USFWS prevented action being taken.[10] To say that Childers, and presumably the men and women he represented who were managing cattle within or on the periphery of the territory being used by the Imnaha wolves, were upset would be a gross understatement.

In response to these frustrations and concerns the ODFW began sending regular text message alerts with information on the whereabouts of the wolves to area ranchers. The location data was pulled from the GPS collars worn by several wolves within the pack, and in offering it to ranchers, the ODFW was in many ways extending an olive branch of trust to the community. The texting system was put into effect on April 16, 2011, and by the thirtieth, the ODFW had sent twenty-eight text messages to area ranchers. In this same time frame the ODFW had also contacted ranchers concerned about depredation in their areas more than one hundred times to provide specific information about the location of the Imnaha wolves in relation to livestock. For the department, the alert system and subsequent follow-up conversations were incredibly resource intensive, but for ranchers the texts were a tool that offered a feeling of control that many in the community had felt was lacking.

Building from the success of the text alert system, ODFW agents, in cooperation with a local livestock producer, instigated a range rider project, and a local cowboy swung into the saddle on April 20, 2011. He carried with him a receiver to use in tracking the radio collars worn by the Imnaha wolves, and the ODFW created maps of GPS coordinates showing recent locations of the pack. On his second day on the job, the cowboy successfully located and hazed five wolves away from grazing livestock, according to reports by the ODFW. The rest of April passed quickly, with the range rider working eight of the ten days left in the month. Despite his presence, however, a depredation was reported and confirmed as a wolf kill on April 30, 2011. The USFWS was the primary investigator. A few days later a dead calf was found on private land. The ODFW incident report stated: "ODFW was not invited to the scene of the dead calf, but later examined the carcass remains of the calf. The muscle hemorrhage along the top of the neck and back and on hind legs clearly showed that trauma was inflicted while the calf was alive (thus, it was a depredation and not scavenging of an already dead calf). The determination that wolves depredated the calf was based on the location and size of the pre-mortem bite marks on the calf. The determination was also supported by the proximity of known Imnaha pack wolves to the kill site."

The ODFW confirmed the calf as a wolf depredation, and the owner of the land where the calf was found requested that the ODFW kill the offending wolves. In response, on May 5, 2011, the same day the decision was made to remove wolves from protection under the federal ESA and restore management authority to the states, the ODFW reviewed the depredations of the last week, the steps taken by area landowners to prevent depredation, and its own efforts to protect livestock. The department then concluded that the situation qualified as chronic depredation under the OWP and began planning for the lethal removal of two wolves from the Imnaha pack.

Beginning the afternoon of May 5, the ODFW worked in collaboration with landowners affected by the Imnaha pack to track and locate the wolves that had been identified for removal. On May 17, agents killed a young male wolf after trapping it on private land where a previous depredation had occurred. On May 18, a female was killed, again on private land in close proximity to a previous depredation site, while at the same time another cow was confirmed to have been killed by a wolf. One day later, the wolf OR-4 was found in an ODFW-placed trap. OR-4's collar had malfunctioned and Morgan replaced it with a GPS collar before releasing the wolf unharmed. In roughly this same time frame, May 5 to May 30, the ODFW also issued permits to twenty-eight

Litigation

June 2011 started off with another cow killed by a wolf from the Imnaha pack. A state-issued order for lethal removal of the wolf was delivered on the same day the depredation was confirmed. The ODFW spent the following three weeks tracking and conducting low-elevation flyovers in an execution patrol for any uncollared members of the Imnaha pack. None were found. The wolves had seemingly disappeared into the high country for the summer without leaving as much as a footprint behind. It was a reprieve that lasted three months.

On September 22, 2011, biologists from the ODFW were called to investigate a possible livestock depredation on private land within the Imnaha pack's known territory. By the time Morgan and his team arrived at the scene the carcass to be investigated was hardly recognizable as a calf. Dead no more then two days, the animal had been almost completely consumed. The little that was left—mostly tufts of hair and bits of tissue—formed sticky rust-colored puddles across a trampled grassy area roughly the size of a city block. Reports from the investigation described a trail of blood crossing into and out of an old falling-down corral. Wolf tracks of varying size wove back and forth across the area, following the gore, winding in circles, spaced close together at first, then farther apart, indicating a chase. The remaining cattle in the area were wide eyed and agitated. They startled at the wind and stood unnaturally huddled together, with their flanks pushing against one another and their heads in the air. Their wet nostrils flared.

Morgan determined wolves from the Imnaha pack had killed the calf roughly forty-eight hours earlier. Data mined from the GPS collar worn by OR-4, the pack's alpha male, confirmed his presence at the scene during that time. OR-2, the alpha female, was also linked to the kill, and after the investigation of the calf's death was complete, Morgan detected radio signals from her collar. Following these signals, he was able to visually identify OR-2 as she loitered near the kill site, then slipped into the thick forest of a nearby canyon.

The loss of the calf marked the fourteenth livestock kill by the Imnaha pack. After confirming the depredation, Morgan and his superiors at the department made the decision to target OR-4 and an uncollared wolf from the Imnaha pack for lethal removal and sought permission from the state Wildlife Commission. The decision would reduce the pack to two animals: OR-2 and a pup born in spring 2011. "We took the decision of lethal removal very seriously and considered it a last resort in line with the management plan," said Morgan. "Livestock owners throughout the area had been using numerous nonlethal measures in their efforts to avoid depredation on their private lands, but the targeted animals were a continuing problem."

Within twenty-four hours of making the request Morgan received the state's go-ahead to hunt and shoot the wolves. On the morning of September 23, he followed the signals from OR-4's GPS collar and spotted the big male, but he could not find a clean shot and did not fire his gun.

Meanwhile, the ODFW's decision to remove another wolf from the state's population was met with widespread concern and disbelief, especially from communities west of the Cascades. The not-for-profit conservation group Oregon Wild began rallying stakeholders and petitioning the governor's office with demands to halt what it deemed the unnecessary and wrongful killing of wolves. "At that point there were people chaining themselves to the doors at ODFW in their efforts to be heard," said Rob Klavins, Oregon Wild's wildlands and wildlife advocate. "Thousands of letters were being sent to the governor's office calling for the protection of wolves and outing the state for its illegal management of an endangered species. They received no response."

Oregon Wild was one of several conservation groups that had waded into the fray that surrounded the creation of the OWP in 2005, and as an organization it had spearheaded a majority of the wolf awareness campaigns and wolf-related political movements in the state. With more than three thousand dues-paying members and a thirty-eight-year history of activism in Oregon, Oregon Wild is a well known, well positioned advocacy group capable of navigating state politics. "We'd been talking to the state for months about how the management plan was being implemented, and about how the managing agencies were failing to honor the compromises the conservation community had agreed to during the creation of the plan," said Klavins. "We received very little response and saw no changes in action."

What Oregon Wild had observed instead, said Klavins, was a state management agency that seemed to cater to the whims and desires of the livestock industry. "Every time there was a dead cow there were people calling for a dead wolf," said Klavins. "And in many cases those requests were granted regardless of whether the situation was in compliance with the wolf plan."

The OWP says all applicable nonlethal controls must by tried prior to lethal removal, and Oregon Wild did not oppose the killing of the wolves involved in the Keating Valley depredations because there was little doubt that the ODFW had followed the plan and made a complete effort to deter the wolves through nonlethal measures, said Klavins. No one in the conservation community was celebrating the decision, but the state had been transparent in the steps taken to prevent additional depredations, and it had tried a variety of different options to protect livestock. "Unfortunately after the Keating event wolf hysteria began to take over parts of the state," said Klavins. "ODFW became much more reactive to political pressure that was being applied by special interest groups via the legislature."

When the depredations occurred in 2010 and the beginning of 2011, Oregon Wild felt the state lacked evidence showing the implementation of nonlethal measures. Part of the problem may have been ambiguity within the OWP itself. The plan lacks measurement criteria that could be used to determine the appropriateness of a response. Part of this vagueness was intentional in order to allow managers to adapt to individual situations, but without benchmarks the appropriateness of nonlethal measures became highly subjective. "They would say they had put up eleven miles of fladry, but they wouldn't say where they had put it, or even if it was at the site of the depredation," said Klavins, talking about the state's implementation of nonlethal measures. "There was no way to know if what they had done was sufficient."

The state in general seemed very uninterested in working with the conservation community in a proactive manner, said Klavins. "They were pretty defensive when we would ask questions, and they would just say they were carrying out the law when they made the wolf kills." According to Klavins, by June 2011, relations between the group and the ODFW had escalated to the point that only high-profile actions would garner a response. "We told them we wanted to work together to find a solution that honored the desires of Oregonians to have native wolves in the state, and to protect endangered species as dictated by the law," said Klavins. "They wanted to fight."

And so the battle began on October 5, 2011, when Oregon Wild, along with two other conservation groups, filed an appeal in the state court requesting a judge to review the state's right to kill a wolf protected under Oregon's endangered species law. In addition, the appeal requested an immediate suspension of the ODFW's authority to carry out the decision to remove the alpha male and one other wolf from the Imnaha pack. The appeal was accepted and a temporary stay granted.

On November 15, 2011, the injunction was extended indefinitely and a lawsuit begun with petitioners Oregon Wild, Cascadia Wildlands, and the Center for Biological Diversity on one side, and respondents ODFW and the Oregon Cattlemen's Association on the other.[1] The petitioners in the case claimed the ODFW was abusing its management authority by killing wolves without giving due attention and diligence to conservation, education, and the adoption of nonlethal management alternatives. While the petitioners had originally been supportive of the plan, their support waned as they suspected the ODFW was responding to political pressure from livestock producers to lethally remove wolves in the state. Their legal challenge argued that the state's management plan runs counter to the Oregon Endangered Species Act, under which wolves in the state are protected.

"The state's management plan requires the exhaustion of all nonlethal options by livestock producers before lethal control be considered," said Nick Cady, the Cascadia Wildlands representing lawyer. "There is no proof that this has occurred. ODFW is saying trust us, trust us, but they've given us no reason to believe they are operating to protect and conserve wolves. What we're seeing is the agency responding to the ranching community and livestock interests, not to the public will."

The lawsuit comes down to whether the state has the legal authority to kill an animal identified as endangered under Oregon's Endangered Species Act, added Klavins. "Regardless of what the wolf plan may say, we believe the state is acting illegally, and we believe the court will side with conservation."

"We did not want to take this to court and create a winner-take-all battle," said Klavins. "If anything we believe the wolf plan should be strengthened, but they weren't willing to sit at the table with us. Looking back in fifty years, no one is ever going to say we wished we would have killed more wolves because now we don't have enough cows."

Since the initial granting of the court-ordered stay, more than twenty additional livestock depredations have occurred, according to ODFW investigations. The number and pattern of the kills suggest a change in the pack's behavior. Initially, smaller calves were targeted and only in the spring and fall. Recent depredations have included mature cows and bulls, and they have occurred outside of the traditional time frame of depredations. "The problem wolves in the Imnaha pack are in a cycle of chronic depredation, and once they get to this point there's no stopping them," said Morgan. "Nonlethal measures have been implemented and proven unsuccessful. Under the management plan approved by the state, the appropriate response at this point is lethal removal, but that option is off the table due to litigation. It's incredibly frustrating for wildlife managers and livestock producers."

The timeline for the resolution of the injunction is currently unknown, and the lawsuit requires a thorough examination of state wildlife protection and management laws. Several groups, including the Oregon Cattlemen's Association and the ODFW, have asked the court to reconsider its ruling claiming a potential for devastating livestock losses and the exacerbation of problem behavior within the Imnaha pack. The court has been unresponsive, and a proposed piece of legislation, dubbed the "kill bill" by conservation groups, that would have amended the state's management plan and restored the ODFW's ability to control for wolves under very specific criteria failed to pass during the 2012 legislative session. However, a wolf compensation bill did pass in the legislature. The compensation bill allocated $100,000 to be distributed by county committees to livestock producers suffering confirmed losses of livestock or dogs. This compensation measure comes in addition to a $5,000 fund with which the State Court of Appeals ordered the petitioners in the lawsuit to cover potential livestock losses occurring during the course of litigation.

All of this calls into question the state's political stance on wolves, the protection offered under the state's ESA and management plan, and the rights of livestock producers to protect their property.

Fourteen years ago, ten years before wolves began to reestablish populations in Oregon, a poll of Oregonians suggested more than half of the population was in favor of protecting wolves. However, because of how the human population is dispersed across the state, it is likely that the majority of people in favor of promoting and protecting wolves live in population centers that are largely outside the realm of wolf activity. In fact, 96 percent of the population lives in areas of the state where the probability of a wolf encounter anytime in the next decade is slim to none. "There is an urban-rural divide that shows up clearly in the wolf issue, but most of the time people only think about it going in one direction with rural communities on the losing side," said Klavins. "Regardless of zip code, we all have a right to wildness. Not living in Wallowa County does not remove our interest, or our right, in caring for and defending native species."

It is inaccurate to say there are no proponents of wolves in eastern Oregon. However, the number of wolf supporters within the populations of Wallowa, Union, Harney, and other eastern Oregon counties is disproportionately lower than in counties with large urban population centers. The reasons behind this disparity are myriad, but they may begin with fear. Fear of change, of financial crises, of outsiders dictating how things should be done, of the dark, of the unknown, and of the big bad wolf himself. Some of these fears are rational. Some are not.

The majority of the antiwolf rhetoric coming out of eastern Oregon originates in ranching communities with strong ties to the Oregon Cattlemen's Association and other livestock groups. In these areas the use of the public landscape for personal economic gain has long-standing precedent: cattle production brought in more than $414 million in gross income in 2009, according to the USDA National Agricultural Statistics Service, and was the top agricultural activity in the eastern portion of the state. The idea, true or not, that wolves could force changes to the status quo and negatively impact the earning ability of ranchers in the region has been a hard pill to swallow for many longtime residents.[2]

"I'm not against wolves," said Karl Patton, who believes he's lost several more cows to wolves since the confirmed depredations of his animals in 2011. "They're just following their nature, being wolves. What's frustrating to me is how we're being forced to deal with them." If his hands and the hands of the state managers continue to be tied, Patton said he sees a real threat to his ranch. "If this keeps going and we're not allowed to do anything, survival is going to be selling everything and giving up on cows," he said. "That's not much of an option."

This is a gross dramatization, said Klavins. Wolves do take down livestock, but the compensation bills are in place to cover the cost of the loss, and the losses to wolves are minimal when compared to all the other ways cattle die. "The negative impact of wolves is blown out of proportion to the problem, and the hysteria doesn't benefit anyone," said Klavins. "There is not an inherent conflict between humans and wildlife. If your business model depends on killing an endangered species, than that's an outdated model."

This division of interests and opinions by geography and politics may be at the root of the human conflict surrounding wolves in Oregon. Though most are too polite to come out and say it, there exists the assumption that the east side of the state is filled with cowboys and rednecks who would rather shoot their neighbor than admit wolves might have a place in the landscape, while the west side contains a bunch of patchouli-wearing, vegetarian hippies that wouldn't know a wolf if it jumped off their T-shirt and pissed on their shoes. State wildlife managers and scientists are caught between these caricatures with very little room to maneuver.

"The whole lawsuit is a disaster," said Daniel Edge, who after helping to write the OWP, spent two terms as the chair of the state's Wildlife Commission. "Right now, the only thing happening is that the plaintiffs are building enemies. There will be no winning."

When the OWP was created, the commission attempted due diligence in its pursuit of a fair and open process that gave equal standing to all involved stakeholders, said Edge. While it wasn't perfect, the plan was a large step forward in managing wolves for their conservation in Oregon. The filing of the lawsuit effectively takes all the teeth from the plan and removes the state's ability to manage the population in a manner that is suitable to the overall goals for conservation. "No biologist wants to have to kill a wolf that is chronically preying on livestock," said Edge. "But the alternative is to do nothing and let the problem continue to build. The management of any species must allow for the removal of individuals when necessary. The lawsuit fails to recognize that it's the population as a whole that must be maintained."

According to the appeal filed with the court, the petitioners in the suit believe the removal of the two Imnaha pack wolves will cause them irreparable harm "because members of their organizations wish to have the 'profound and exhilarating' experience of viewing wolves in the wild, including the particular wolves targeted for killing." They also contend that as membership advocacy organizations representing thousands of Oregonians who regularly provide monetary donations to their causes, they have a substantial interest in the reestablishment of a viable wolf population in Oregon.

Complicating the matter is the deceptively tricky issue of determining the actual size of the state's wolf population. Parties from both sides of the lawsuit disagree on the number of wolves in Oregon. At the time of filing, the petitioners contended there were only about fourteen wolves, the ODFW said twenty-three, and the Oregon Cattlemen's Association claimed thirty-four, with nine or ten lone wolves. Not in dispute were the approximately fifty-five thousand cattle and calf deaths in Oregon in 2010, the last year for which records are available. According to the plaintiffs, 94 percent of those fatalities were from nonpredator causes (such as digestive and respiratory problems, calving problems, weather, theft, and poisoning), and of the remaining 6 percent attributed to predators, between 63 percent of cows and 70 percent of calves were killed by coyotes, 13 percent of cows and 8 percent of calves by mountain lions, 7 percent of cows by bears, 7 percent of calves by wolves, 0.5 percent of calves by dogs, and the remaining losses by unknown predators. Cady, speaking for Cascadia Wildlands, said that given these numbers and the small size of the existing wolf population, killing even two wolves would irreparably harm the reestablishment of a viable, self-sustaining wolf population in Oregon, while doing little to change the number of cattle deaths across the state.

Bullshit, calls Edge from his office at Oregon State University, where he's head of the Department of Fisheries and Wildlife and has been part of the faculty since 1989. The conservation plan is about doing what needs to be done to get enough animals on the landscape so that they can be delisted and their protection under the state's Endangered Species Act removed. Fourteen stakeholder groups agreed on a two-pronged approach focused on conservation and tolerance. Allowing the state to kill problem wolves is an important element in building human tolerance. Without management tools that include lethal removal we will likely see livestock producers losing confidence and patience with the state, said Edge. It's increasingly likely that we will see the vigilante removal of wolves from the landscape regardless of whether or not they have harmed livestock. "If we can manage as planned, we will be delisting wolves within ten years, and possibly within five," said Edge. "Now that they're here, Oregon will continue to have wolves. Their biology is such that they can survive almost all attempts to remove them from a landscape. When stressed they breed like rodents."

While the lawsuit has called a halt to the ODFW's ability to kill wolves, livestock producers do retain their use of state-issued "caught-in-the-act" permits to control for depredating wolves. "Ranchers should have a right to protect their property, and lethal control is part of every management plan," said Morgan, while noting that the likelihood of a rancher killing a wolf under the conditions outlined by the permits is slim. "Wolf biology is going to make it very difficult for livestock producers to control for depredation on their own. We're in a very hard place."

The wolf characteristics to which Morgan is referring are their propensity to hunt at night, to travel long distances in search of prey, and to learn which livestock deterrents pose a threat and which are merely smoke and mirrors. These things are the rock. The public response to wolves and our understanding of wildlife management is the hard place.

The Problems of Retribution

It's 6:55 a.m. on April 11, 2012. I'm meeting Rod Childers at the Friends diner in downtown Enterprise in five minutes. I've been camping out in Wallowa County for several days, and I spend the extra time tucking in my shirt and trying to get my hair to stop sticking up in the back. Looking into my rearview mirror I realize it's no help, and I tell myself to buy a hairbrush before my next meeting. I doubt that looking like I've been sleeping in the dirt is going to get me far in a place where creased Wranglers and scuffed cowboy boots are the daily uniform for a majority of the population, and "environmentalists" are being accused of destroying a way of life.

The injunction on lethal removal of wolves in Oregon remains active, and a few weeks ago, the ODFW announced the cessation of the text messaging system it had put into place to help keep livestock producers aware of the movement of wolves around their animals. The announcement and the decision to stop the texts, coupled with the continued "allowed killing of livestock," has cast a pall over everything wolf related, and I fear that even at Friends question-asking writers may not be welcomed with open arms.

Pulling open the diner's door I'm hit with the warm smells of coffee and hash browns. As I step into the dining room where a long table is half-filled with people I can only guess have been meeting here for coffee for the last thirty years, conversation stops. I'm the youngest person in the room by at least two decades. Standing at the foot of the table is a stocky, barrel-chested man in a worn white cowboy hat. He had been laughing when I walked in, and he's still smiling when he looks me up and down. "You must be Aimee," he says, holding out his hand. His palm and fingertips are thick with calluses, and he shakes my hand firmly, as if testing my mettle.

I follow Childers into the deserted back dining room, where we sit across from one another at a table that could have come straight from a country grandmother's kitchen. I can tell he's still sizing me up when he asks about my background. I stop myself from tugging on the end of my ponytail and instead begin to tell him my story and why I'm out in Enterprise. After fifteen minutes, he remains a bit skeptical but seems willing to trust that I'm not a wolf-loving, rancher-hating environmentalist from Portland out to wreck his life and the lives of everyone he knows. Despite his gruff front Childers seems passionate and kind, and when the waitress comes by the second time to ask if we're finally ready to order, I take a moment to bow my head and silently hope that I can talk about wolves in Oregon without betraying the ranchers, the wolves, or my own beliefs. In the political climate out here, that seems to mean walking a line as fine as the barbed wire fencing that unfurls across the Wallowa Valley. The waitress turns to me and I follow Childers's lead, ordering a waffle with maple syrup.

For the next hour Childers gives me his perspective on state government: "Four counties decide how the state is run." The biggest issue in wolf management: "Politics." And the impact the state-employed range rider had on preventing depredation by wolves: "He was a coroner reporting kills more than he was a preventive force."

Childers has been ranching in Wallowa County for most of his adult life. He currently runs about four hundred cow/calf pairs on his ranch near Joseph. He has sat on several natural resource–oriented committees in Wallowa County, including the Grande Ronde Model Watershed Program and the county's Natural Resource Advisory Board, and he currently heads the Oregon Cattlemen's Association Wolf Task Force. As was the case when Karl Patton lost his two cows, Childers is often the first person other ranchers in the area call when they have a problem they believe involves wolves.

"Proof is everything," says Childers, who has eaten half his waffle and pushed the rest aside. "You can tell the state you have a wolf problem all day long, and unless you show up with a cow with a wolf still attached you're not going to get much help." Childers also says that in 80 percent of the investigations in 2011, the ODFW said the kill was not wolf related, and 80 percent of the time people disagreed with them based on their own career experience dealing with predators.

These investigations were after May 5, 2011, when the ODFW was still actively managing depredation through the implementation of nonlethal methods and lethal control and before the legal injunction. Despite this, Childers insists there were many more wolf depredations than the department was willing to admit. "Wildlife services, the sheriff's office, the vet's office, will all say, 'Yes that's a wolf,' but in terms of getting the rancher compensated, or the wolf removed, it's ODFW that counts, and they'll say 'No, it's something else,'" says Childers, adding that at a certain point livestock producers are going to stop calling for help and start taking care of what they see as their problems on their own.

"We're honest law-abiding citizens, but we do believe we have rights," he says. "We're trying to work through this." Childers pauses. He doesn't invoke the shoot, shovel, and shut up doctrine, but it sits between us on the table. Finally, reaching for the bill, he says, "You do what you have to do."

Two months after my conversation with Childers at Friends, Tabitha Viner, a veterinary pathologist with the USFWS's National Wildlife Forensics Lab, is recreating the process involved in performing a necropsy on a wolf killed by unknown causes. Imagine this:

A wolf carcass lies supine in a spread-eagle position on a cold metal table. It's a male. Viner, clad in surgical gown and gloves, has just opened the body's main cavity by using a large scalpel to make an incision that begins at the chin, travels the length of the torso, and ends inches from the anus at the pubis. Earlier she had taken an X-ray of the remains and gone over the films looking for broken and damaged bones. She had also gone over the outside of the carcass, squeezing the limbs and checking the trunk for abnormalities and wounds the same way a paramedic would examine an accident victim at the scene of a car crash. She had combed through the pelt, examining the hair for signs of singeing, the skin for inflammation and discoloration. She had checked the mouth, making note of any broken teeth before looking at the eyes and ears. Now she was ready to skin the entire animal. "Bullet holes can be as small as five millimeters in diameter," said Viner. "They are often hidden under the hair. With the skin off, you can see any damage."[1]

After removing the pelt and examining it, Viner goes over the remains once again. She looks at the feet, paying careful attention to any damage in the muscles. She takes copious notes that will read much like a coroner's report from a human crime scene. Once she finishes with the outside of the animal, she delves into the innards. Removing the heart, lungs, kidneys, and other major organs, Viner checks each one over individually. She slices the mahogany-colored liver like a loaf of bread in order to better study its consistency and texture. "Poison would likely show up in the liver," she said.

The stomach gets its own inspection. From it Viner gathers information about the wolf's diet premortem. By looking at the level of decomposition of the stomach's contents, she can tell roughly when the last meal was eaten. When she completes the macrolevel investigations of the organs, she takes a series of tissue samples that will be used to perform additional diagnostic tests to identify the presence of bacteria and viruses. Finally, Viner saws open the skull and removes the brain.

"Our end goal is to figure out the cause of death for that specific animal," said Viner. "We're looking for the story of the death. Sometimes it's undetermined, and sometimes it's very clear." If a wolf dies of a gunshot wound, in addition to finding a hole, Viner said she would usually see an explosion of bullet fragments inside the animal. In the forensics world, it's called a lead snowstorm.

According to the federal Endangered Species Act, intentionally harming or killing any animal protected by the law is a crime punishable by jail time and fines up to $100,000. Viner's work assists federal and state wildlife law enforcement officers in their investigation of potential violations of wildlife law. Since 2000, the ODFW in cooperation with the USFWS has sent several wolves found dead in Oregon to the forensics lab for investigation to determine the cause of death.[2]

Backtrack now two years to August 4, 2010. Morgan has finally succeeded in trapping a wolf from the Wenaha pack. The wolf is a two-year-old male, weighing ninety-seven pounds and in good overall condition. Morgan worked with agents from the Umatilla National Forest and the US Forest Service to track and radio-collar the wolf. Trapping the wolf had been a three-year process that began when the Wenaha wolves had responded to Morgan's howls in the middle of the night.

Collaring the wolf, documented as OR-6, will have a significant impact on the ODFW's ability to track and monitor the pack and should help the state make more accurate population estimates for management purposes. Estimates based on tracks and reported sightings suggested the Wenaha pack had four adults, but the presence of pups was uncertain. At the time OR-6 was captured, there were likely fewer than fifteen wolves in the state divided between two packs. "This is an important milestone in monitoring the Wenaha pack," said Morgan at the time of capture. "Now, we will be able to determine specific use areas of this pack, pack numbers, and pup production."

Now it is almost two months later, September 30, 2010, and an Oregon State University student working with the ODFW wolf program as a summer intern finds OR-6 dead in a forested area of the Wenaha drainage. The student had been part of the team that had captured and collared OR-6. She was incredibly shaken when she called to report she'd found him, said Morgan. "It was a terrible thing."

The federal Endangered Species Act should have protected OR-6. If his death was human caused it was in direct violation of federal law. The USFWS Office of Law Enforcement began an investigation of the case. The agency sent OR-6's remains to the Wildlife Forensics Lab in Ashland, Oregon, then issued a press release offering a $2,500 reward for any information related to the case. The release did not make public any information related to a potential cause of death, but speculation across multiple media outlets suggested OR-6 had been shot by a poacher.

Within hours of the USFWS announcement, a cadre of conservation groups joined together and put up an additional $7,500 for information related to OR-6's death, bringing the total reward offered to $10,000. The groups included were the Hells Canyon Preservation Council, Oregon Wild, the Center for Biological Diversity, Defenders of Wildlife, The Humane Society of the United States, The Humane Society Wildlife Land Trust, and Northeast Oregon Ecosystems. In a statement to the Associated Press, Greg Dyson, the executive director of the Hells Canyon Preservation Council, said, "There's room for both wolves and ranching, but there have got to be above-the-board efforts to make it work. We've been concerned by some of the public statements leaders from other groups have made that are strongly anti-wolf. We're concerned that they have been incendiary and may have encouraged someone to take the law into their own hands."

Four months pass. No new information is presented.

Wally Sykes, a Wallowa County resident and the founder of the Northeast Oregon Ecosystems group, becomes frustrated by the lack of progress in the case. Using the relationships built when the news of the investigation first broke, Sykes organizes the purchase of advertising space on a billboard located along Highway 82 eastbound. In letters several feet tall, the sign reads "WHO KILLED THE WENAHA WOLF?" It then gives information about the reward and a phone number for the USFWS. At the bottom of the sign, painted in red, is the statement "WHATEVER YOU THINK ABOUT WOLVES, POACHING IS WRONG."

In a press release put out by one of the conservation groups offering reward money, Sykes is quoted as saying, "Just like in Yellowstone, the return of wolves to Oregon has the potential to draw visitors from all over the country. Anti-wildlife attitudes and rhetoric that result in the illegal killing of endangered species are counterproductive and give our community a black eye."

The billboard stands for a single day before the owner of the land on which the sign stands calls the company responsible for its management and requests the ad be removed. It is replaced with a picture of a snarling wolf and the nonsensical text "Wolves are protected, why not cows, people, and private property rights?"

In an essay that runs in *High Country News* a few months after the billboard fiasco, Mitch Wolgamott, a trained biologist and lifelong Oregonian living in Union County, writes, "Misleading rhetoric in these emotionally charged debates only serves to rally extremists on both sides while alienating and confusing the more thoughtful—and numerous—middle ground where the solutions reside. The placement on a billboard of a huge and snarling wolf head next to text falsely implying that property rights are being taken away is guaranteed to heat the blood of many Westerners. It does nothing to resolve differences between wolf advocates and opponents."

Wolgamott had hit the nail on the head, but the public debate and the response to wolves only grew hotter and more convoluted.

The Media Circus

In fall 2011, as Oregon went to court over the proposed lethal removal of the two Imnaha wolves, another wolf story was unfolding. OR-7, a two-year-old male wolf, had left eastern Oregon and was making his way west.

Part of the first known litter of pups born to the Imnaha pack, OR-7 had been captured by an ODFW team in February 2011 and fitted with a GPS collar. As he traveled away from the pack, biologists were able to follow his movements via the satellite technology and they quickly identified OR-7 as a dispersing wolf likely looking for a mate and new territory. However, unlike many dispersing wolves, OR-7 did not seem content to travel only past the borders of his home territory and no farther. Instead he seemed to make use of the patchwork of wilderness and roadless areas that exist across Oregon. He followed a path that hopscotched hundreds of miles from the Eagle Cap Wilderness and went into areas where wolves remained protected by the federal Endangered Species Act in addition to the state act. "The protected wilderness areas and wild lands acted as migration corridors for OR-7 to use as he traveled on a southwest path through the state," said Nick Cady, whose work at Cascadia Wildlands includes campaigns to protect and restore wilderness areas in the state. "Many of the areas he traveled through were designated as wilderness and therefore did not have grazing livestock. His path showed that there are areas where wolves can travel and exist without conflict."

In the last week of October, after traveling through the Soda Mountain Wilderness, the Sky Lakes Wilderness, and the area surrounding Crater Lake National Park, OR-7 crossed State Highway 97 and the crest of the Cascade Range to enter Douglas County in southwestern Oregon, bringing him within a stone's throw of the area where the last wolf in Oregon had been killed for bounty money in 1946. His arrival on the west side of the state sparked new debate that ranged from celebratory to hostile.

The Medford-based Oregon Hunters Association, which opposed the reestablishment of wolves in the state from the get-go, told local news media they feared that OR-7 and the wolves that would likely follow him into western Oregon would harm the region's deer and elk populations, which were already suffering from cougar predation. On the other side a spokesperson for Big Wildlife, a regional conservation group, was quoted as saying, "The people needed to embrace wolves as an apex predator that would help restore an ecological balance to the landscape."

As OR-7 continued to explore the area, he crossed back and forth over the Cascade Range. One day his collar would ping in Klamath County, the next it would show up in Douglas County. He was a wolf on the move, and on December 28, 2011, he crossed into northern California. Unsurprisingly, OR-7's arrival in the Golden State sent the global media into frenzy. News of his travels appeared on MSNBC, in *Time* magazine, the *San Francisco Chronicle*, the Associated Press, Reuters, and thousands of other outlets. The story grew even larger when a hunter found an image of OR-7 on a game camera he had placed along a remote trail deep in the forest. While it could not be verified with 100 percent certainty that the wolf in the image was OR-7, the ODWF did confirm that according to information from his collar, OR-7 had been in the area when the picture was taken and it "seemed likely" that the wolf depicted was indeed OR-7. It was official—like a true star, OR-7 had been photographed without his knowledge, and the image went viral.

In a statement to the *San Francisco Chronicle*, Amaroq Weiss, who had been part of Oregon's Wolf Advisory Committee prior to taking a position with the California Wolf Center, said, "This is probably the most significant conservation story for this state and this species in decades. To have a wolf set foot in the state when the last one was killed in 1924 is spectacularly big news."

While wolves in Oregon had been receiving semiregular coverage in the news since the OWP was drafted, OR-7's entrance into areas long thought to be outside wolf territory truly brought the reality of wolves into many homes for the first time. In an attempt to capitalize on this newfound public awareness, Oregon Wild initiated a contest for children and teenagers to rename OR-7. It wasn't the first time the conservation group had taken steps to personalize and humanize a dispersing wolf. In 2009, efforts had been made to rename OR-2 as "Sophie"; however, that campaign was largely unsuccessful. With OR-7 the group was determined to gain traction with the public, openly admitting that the contest was part of an effort to make the wolf "too famous to kill." The group solicited schools around the globe, asking them to have their students submit suggestions for names. More than 250 submissions were received, from which Oregon Wild selected five finalists.[1] After ten days of voting and the counting of more than seven hundred ballots, the group announced OR-7 would be christened "Journey." Several months later, "Journey" hadn't stuck around, but OR-7 was still roaming the hills of northern California, likely in search of a mate who hadn't yet arrived.

The naming, which people on all sides of the wolf debate agree was a publicity stunt, is only a small and relatively innocuous sample of the steps people in the state have been willing to take to garner support for their side of the wolf debate.

The first time I met Russ Morgan we sat across from one another at a table designed for twenty in the conference room of the ODFW office in La Grande, Oregon. On the table were huge blown-up maps of the wildlife management units where the department knew, or suspected, wolves were living. The maps showed property ownership boundaries, roads and rivers, and forest coverage, as well as information pertaining to the wolves' den sites, meeting points, and locations at which depredations had occurred. Roblyn Brown, the assistant wolf coordinator, came in as I was settling into my chair, and working quickly she cleared most of the documents from the table. It was sensitive material, and the department had been plagued with inaccurate news stories, grossly slanted editorials, and half-true political statements meant to portray wolves and Oregon's wolf population as something they weren't. Morgan and Brown didn't want to be responsible for potentially fueling another bout of flawed reporting. Who could blame them.

Erroneous, poorly reported, and made-up "facts" that have more to do with fairy tales than science have become standard fare in society's rapidly developing digital era. Suddenly anyone with an Internet connection and Facebook account can be an expert on wolf biology and management. There are few checks and balances in place to stop the viral spread of information, regardless of its truth. "News media are attracted to controversy, and wolf recovery, depredations, control programs, and most any other wolf topics seem irresistible," wrote wolf biologists Steven Fritts, Robert Stephenson, Robert Hayes, and Luigi Boitani in their work on wolves and humans.[2] "Popular information about wolves is often biased or inaccurate. When wolf stories appear, the extreme views of opponents and supporters of wolves are often highlighted, further polarizing the issue."

In addition to the issues in traditional media, the digital world has helped to foster huge interest in wolves, said Morgan. While it's good the public is involved and wants to know more about the natural world, little fact-checking occurs and many people are often left on their own to determine what is real and what is fiction. "I can find more misinformation about wolves on a given day than I can accurate information," said Morgan. "In the six years I've been here I've addressed more questions on tapeworm, reintroduction, and Canadian gray wolves than I ever thought would be possible."

For the record, the tapeworm Morgan is referring to is called *Echinococcus granulosus*. It's a natural part of a wolf's (and dog's) ecology and does not pose a significant risk to humans. However, to prevent transmission, gloves should be worn by anyone handling dog or wolf feces. The reintroduction Morgan mentions has already been discussed, but to recap, the only reintroduction that has occurred was federally sanctioned and carried out in Idaho and parts of Montana, including Yellowstone National Park. Wolves entered Oregon through natural dispersal. Finally, the populations of wolves in southern Canada, the northern US Rockies, interior British Columbia, the Northwest Territories, and nearly all of Alaska are closely related. They belong to a single subspecies known as *Canis lupus occidentalis.*

Morgan's experience in dealing with misinformation and issues of inadequate education is par for the course when it comes to wolves. Throughout the West, wolf managers and biologists have been placed in the unenviable position of middlemen, and while their first task is most often to implement state-approved plans, they often spend an inordinate amount of time in the public spotlight as controversy builds around them.[3] Historically, Morgan and his peers have received the most criticism and attention from antiwolf groups, but in the last fifteen years the paradigm has shifted and prowolf groups have become just as vocal and just as outraged as their counterparts.

"Very few people in modern times have had a personal interaction with a wolf," said Oregon biologist Mark Henjum. "But for many people just the thought of wolves is enough to elicit a powerful response." Henjum recalls looking out over a sea of cowboy hats at an early town hall meeting held in the high school gymnasium in Enterprise, Oregon. The focus was strictly on providing information and answering questions, yet people were upset to the point where Henjum said he was concerned about the potential for physical violence between audience members. "We had several plainclothes policemen in the audience, and after one prowolf person spoke, I turned to an officer and told him it was his job to make sure the speaker made it home safe," said Henjum. "People would show up to the events intoxicated, and several prowolf supporters in rural areas have been subjected to intimidation and ostracism."

According to recent studies by David Mech and other biologists, the last twenty years have seen an increase in public support of wolves. However, it has not been distributed equally across society. The response by many rural livestock producers in eastern Oregon has been typical of what researchers have observed throughout the West, where the closer people live to wolves the less likely they are to feel positive toward the species. Among farmers and ranchers living in areas near wolves, negative feelings prevail.

These views are rooted in many concerns, including attacks on livestock, danger to domestic animals and humans, costs associated with management, declines in large game due to predation, the potential negation of private property rights, and regulatory changes to private use of federal land. In contrast, people living in cities and urban areas and members of environmental organizations hold the most positive and supportive views of wolves. In support of their stance, this group often cites the role wolves can play in ecosystem health, the inherent right of wildlife to exist, and the added value wolves give to recreational wilderness experiences.[4]

This variance in attitudes and concerns is to be expected when dealing with different segments of society, but the level to which each group has risen in support of their ideals has in many cases straddled a line between polite fervor and evangelical madness.

Throughout recent memory, the fear wolves instigate has largely been out of proportion to the threat wolves create for humanity. The view individuals have taken of wolves has largely been created by the culture they live within. As wolf biologist Luigi Boitani explains it, "There is the wolf as science can describe it, but there is also the wolf that is a product of the human mind, a cultural construct—sometimes called the 'symbolic wolf'—colored by our individual, cultural, or social conditioning."[5]

Wallowa County rancher Karl Patton tells a story about the time a few years ago when wolves almost ate him, his dogs, and his cows. It was around 3:30 a.m. in March. There was still snow on the ground, but many of Patton's animals had already given birth, and the young calves were out in the pasture with the cows. Patton was in bed with his wife in his ranch house just outside Joseph, Oregon, when the dogs "just started going nuts." He woke immediately to the noise. It wasn't normal barking; he could tell the dogs were after something.

Patton grabbed his pistol and cell phone, jumped into his coveralls and boots, and ran out of the house. His dogs met him at the door. They'd been chased by something and only one of them had any interest in going back out to the pasture where Patton had sixty head contained. Patton ran into the darkness, the moon lighting the way. About a hundred yards from the house, the length of a football field minus the end zones, he saw the wolves. They were coming right at him. Four or five of them, maybe six. A couple started trying to work their way behind him. They were trying to get between him and the house. He fired his gun. Then fired it again. He didn't aim, just pulled the trigger.

"The flash from the muzzle left me night-blind," he said. "I just kept shooting and yelling trying to drive them off." The wolves turned and ran. Adrenaline pumping, Patton dialed 911, then the Oregon Cattlemen's Association's Rod Childers. Childers lived nearby, and Patton wanted confirmation of whatever he was about to see. When he reached his animals they were bunched together in a corner so tight that he couldn't move between them. He kept looking for a dead animal, but there wasn't one. The only things marring the snow were the wolf tracks, some as big as his hand.

In the morning the Wallowa County sheriff, a USDA Wildlife Services agent, Childers, and Morgan all looked over the scene. "Everyone had to see the same thing at the same time," said Patton. "The wolves had come all the way down to the fence around the yard."

In front of public officials, to newspaper reporters, in writing, and during public talks Patton has told this story several times since it happened. The event had a huge impact on him, and when he talks about it it's clear he's reliving moments from that night. Several times he reiterates how the gun flash blinded him—that he couldn't see where the wolves were, or where they were going. He says again and again that his dogs were going insane, that they ran like crazy for the house, then hid in the barn. Then he says, and this is the crux, he says he felt helpless. Like there was nothing he could do, like his private property was just out there waiting to be taken from him.

Patton is one of the few ranchers in the West to have seen wolves, and the ranching community has used his personal account of the experience as a tool to gain support. More than a year after the incident occurred, Patton stood in front of the Oregon House of Representatives Agriculture and Natural Resources Committee in support of four legislative bills. One was bill 3560, which if passed would establish a compensation fund to reimburse Oregonians who lost livestock to wolves. The other three bills focused on lessening restrictions on killing wolves in the state. After all the testimony was given and the session came to an end, 3560 passed. The other bills did not.

Like OR-7, Patton's story made news in large part because of how it was told. A man stands alone facing the darkness and the unknown in protection of what is his, yet he is powerless to act. In the case of OR-7, a lone wolf travels nearly a thousand miles through wilderness and across mountains into regions from which his species has been absent for more than sixty years. The stories could as easily have been that a man hears his dogs barking in the middle of the night, checks on them, sees a handful of wolves on the edge of his pasture, and fires his gun to scare them away; a naturally dispersing wolf goes out in search of a mate and territory.

By focusing on outlying examples of wolves and wolf interactions in Oregon rather than telling the same old story of the status quo, special interest groups and the media have managed to shape much of the public response to wolves. The result has been the creation of yet more myths, and though they may be entertaining, they are not honest. "Sometimes I think wolves receive the response they do because in many ways there are similarities between wolves and humans," said Morgan. "They operate in a miniature society in packs that resemble family units. They do what they want when they want. They're bold and successful, and they compete for resources we also use."

The Science of Recovery

There is little doubt that wolves are on the path to recovery in Oregon, but it's not a done deal. As a species they continue to face innumerable challenges in the state, including the disappearance and loss of individuals, dispersal to other states, and death from both natural and human causes. Management at this point requires continued monitoring and observation by unbiased scientists. The information collected by these men and women will ultimately benefit both wolf recovery efforts and efforts to improve social tolerance for wolves through the prevention of conflict between wolves and humans and between wolves and domestic animals.

It's 7:00 a.m. in late May 2012 and I'm following two sets of tracks through a snow-covered meadow in the Eagle Cap Wilderness above the Minam River. The prints weren't here last night, and as I walk beside them through open meadows and forested groves I realize they are coming from the ridge where I ate yesterday's peanut butter sandwich and they're heading toward the cabin where Roblyn Brown, the state's assistant wolf coordinator, and I spent the evening tossing and turning in creaking cots that smelled of mice and dust. Based on their size and the length of the stride I know the tracks are wolf.

Last night before lighting a fire and settling in for the night, Brown and I had stood in the meadow beyond the cabin and howled for wolves. Perhaps it was these calls that brought the wolves along this path. Maybe it was the smell of woodsmoke coming from a building that had sat empty and cold through the winter months. Or it could have been the wolves were simply out for a midnight stroll under the light of the moon and were as oblivious to our presence as we were to theirs.

Brown and I had ventured into the Minam after the ODFW received reports of at least one wolf in the area. A team of wildlife biologists tracking wolverines in the drainage had found a picture of what appeared to be a lactating female wolf on one of their heat-sensitive trail cameras. The picture made its way to Brown's office, and after talking it over with Russ Morgan, they decided it would be worthwhile to hike the six miles into the area where the picture had been taken and place a few cameras of their own. The outing would also provide ample time to conduct howling surveys and search for tracks and other signs of wolves.

Before heading out Brown warned me it was unlikely that we'd find much. Late-season snow would make travel difficult, and the sheer size of the Minam watershed meant a lot of potential area for the animals to claim as territory. Also, she said, the female captured by the camera might have just been passing through the drainage. It would take some luck to see anything.

Not far past the cabin the tracks seem to disappear into nothing. I turn around and make my way back to the porch to wait for Brown, who had hiked off in the opposite direction half an hour earlier. She arrives at the cabin shortly after I do, and looking at the grin on her face I can't help but think we should have bought lottery tickets.

Tucked into her right hand, Brown carries the wrapper of the energy bar she'd eaten for breakfast. Folded carefully into the foil is a charcoal briquette–sized chunk of dark black scat and bits of white-tipped hair. She sets the whole package down on a boulder next to the porch and goes inside to retrieve her genetics sampling kit—a handful of tiny test tubes, a lighter, a pair of tweezers, and a permanent marker. After sterilizing the tweezers in the lighter's flame, Brown proceeds to scrape chunks from the outside of the scat and drop them one by one into a test tube. When the tube is about half full, she caps it and labels it, and then wipes the tweezers with a bit of toilet paper before again sterilizing them in the lighter's flame. Everything then gets sealed into a heavy-duty quart-sized Ziploc and placed securely into the cargo pocket on the side of Brown's pants. We find two more scat samples on our way back to the trailhead, and with each one Brown repeats the entire process from start to finish. She's careful and exact. Each scrape of her tweezers collects a potential galaxy of information about the health and overall status of Oregon's wolf population.

Every time the ODFW captures and collars a new wolf, the attending biologists perform a physical of the animal and take a tissue sample for genetic testing. When they find potential wolf sign in areas where they think an unknown wolf may be traveling, they take a sample. Find a den? Sample for hair from pups. Confirmed depredation? Sample for saliva on bite wounds. A pile of scat amid a path of prints? Sample. In the majority of cases these pieces of evidence, the bits of tissue, skin, scat, and hair, are sent to Dr. Lisette Waits at the University of Idaho's Laboratory for Conservation and Ecological Genetics.

Waits is an internationally recognized researcher in the field of predator and large animal genetics. She has worked with grizzly bears in Montana, sharks in the Pacific Ocean, gray wolves in Idaho, Bengal tigers in Nepal, and wolves throughout Alaska and the West. If it's an endangered predator species of a decent size, there's a pretty good chance Waits has looked at its genetic code at one point or another. "We can take one small sample and from it learn a great deal about the population we're studying," said Waits. She compares the process to crime scene investigation. "We're using a hair sample to create a story about how an individual animal came to be somewhere at a certain time."

By performing these investigations in the lab, Waits is hoping to help wildlife managers and field biologists better manage populations and assist in species recovery in the wild. "We look at connectivity and gene flow to detect the level of isolation within a group," said Waits. "We're looking for genetic variation to tell us something about the population."

Entire species of animals become endangered for two primary reasons. Either they lose habitat, or they lose genetic variation.[1] Habitat loss is a relatively straightforward concept; when a species no longer has a place to live or food to eat there's going to be trouble. Loss of genetic variation is trickier and is often the result of inbreeding within a small, isolated population. As closely related individuals mate, the diversity within their genetic code is depleted, and as a result the species becomes less robust. Species recovery requires both adequate habitat, which wolves in Oregon have, and a deep enough genetic pool to ensure adequate variation. This is where Waits enters the picture.

After the mail is opened and the bits of wolf are prepped for testing by placing a small portion of the sample in a chemical solution that breaks it down into proteins and DNA, the rest of what happens in Waits's lab is largely invisible to the naked eye. Once the samples are prepped, DNA from the rest of the cellular material is extracted in a process that lasts three to four hours, said Waits. I picture this as something like straining the cream from the milk, but I imagine it's more like spilling both the salt and pepper shakers across the counter and trying to pick up only the salt. The next step, said Waits, is to identify the species from which the sample originated. The answer may seem obvious, but until the tests are completed most of the samples can only be assumed to be from the expected species. There's rarely proof that supposed wolf scat samples are anything but bits of waste that could have been collected at the local dog park. Waits's whole process is designed to remove the uncertainty of identification and ensure accurate results. To do this, she said, you have to start with the very basic question, "What exactly am I looking at?" The genetic fingerprint of all canids is similar, and domestic dogs are actually the species most closely related to gray wolves, Waits tells me. This close relationship allows for wolf-dog hybridization and also for the dog genome, which was sequenced in 2006, to act as a stand-in for gray wolves.[2]

Once Waits determines the sample is actually wolf, she can begin fine-tuning her investigation to determine where the individual wolf the sample came from originated, which other wolves it might be related to, whether it's an animal that has been accounted for previously, and a slew of other information related to population density and health. "It sounds quick, but it's a long lab process," said Waits. "It can take several weeks to fully analyze a set of samples." Part of the wait has to do with the number of times each sample is studied. At a minimum each test is repeated at least three times and often up to seven. "Overall our results are incredibly accurate," said Waits, adding that each sample the lab runs is deposited in a genetic library that serves to refine the system further.

Genetic testing has been used to monitor the wolf recovery process throughout the West. It's a noninvasive tool managers can use to receive information about dynamic populations of wolves that may range over large areas. In 2010 a study of genetic diversity within the northern Rocky Mountain gray wolf population found that the wolves regularly dispersed and bred across the region at a high enough rate to maintain strong genetic variation even at population levels lower than formerly believed.[3] At the time, it was big news for wildlife managers seeking to maintain base-level populations in line with recovery goals, but according to wildlife biologist Luigi Boitani, while genetic diversity can be lost in small isolated populations, there is as yet no evidence that any wild wolf population has been affected by loss of genetic diversity. That doesn't mean it can be ignored, however, said ODFW's Brown. In wolf populations like Oregon's that are still establishing, there have to be enough animals to support new breeding pairs outside of familial relations.

"In the last decade there have been huge strides made in understanding how species recover," said Mary Curtis, a USFWS geneticist. "There are species where populations had dwindled so low that there wasn't enough genetic diversity to have healthy recovery." To clarify, a larger population usually means increased genetic diversity, but not always. When a population grows without the genetic coffers to ensure a good mixing of genes during mating and reproduction, that population is courting weakness. The population may be getting bigger, but it's all fat and no muscle. "A higher level of genetic diversity is going to give the population an edge for survival," said Curtis.

A few months after Brown and I placed the cameras in the Minam drainage, Russ Morgan spent one of his rare days off hiking in the area. A few hours into his day he heard howls from the Upper Minam River area. Following them, he came across a small lake where two adult wolves and five pups had gathered and seemed to be lounging in the summer sun. "It's not something that happens," said Morgan of the experience. "To be out there not at all looking for wolves and to come across a previously unknown pack is incredibly rare." Morgan's discovery brought the total known number of pups born in Oregon in 2012 to twenty-five, and the number of known reproducing packs to six. These pups nearly doubled the state's entire 2011 population count of both adults and young.

Wolf packs tend to be largest in the late spring and early summer, after pups are born. A few adults and some pups will often die during the summer, with adult mortality peaking in the fall and winter.[4] If at least two pups and both breeding adults from each pack survive through the end of the year, Oregon will count six breeding pairs, and according to the OWP, the state needs only four breeding pairs for three consecutive years in order to remove wolves from protection under the state's Endangered Species Act. It's a significant increase from last year, when the Walla Walla pack was confirmed as the only successful breeding pair in the state. The increased number of packs has already provided the opportunity for greater genetic drift among Oregon's growing wolf population.

Based on test results from genetic samples collected in the spring and summer of 2012, the ODFW was able to confirm the movement of individual wolves into new and established packs, where it was assumed mating and reproduction would occur. Those results showed that a wolf from the Wenaha pack dispersed, possibly into the Sled Springs area; OR-12, the breeding male for the Wenaha pack, was born into the Imnaha pack; and OR-10 and OR-11 from the Walla Walla pack are full siblings with no known close relations to the other Oregon packs. Previous testing for the state had also confirmed the presence of three wolves with genetic ties to Idaho's Snake River pack living as part of the Wenaha pack. Two of those wolves were brothers but seemingly not related to any other Oregon wolves. Another sample collected in the Mount Emily area outside La Grande, Oregon, showed the presence of a female wolf that did not share any relationship to other Oregon wolves. The diversity of genetic material represented by these unrelated wolves when coupled with the overall number of animals will likely be a key factor in the recovery of the species in the state.

In an article on the *Smithsonian* magazine's website, Alistair Bland wrote, "The wolf situation in Oregon is extraordinary because the animals are coming back on their own—a rare example of a large predator actually expanding its range instead of, as is the more common pattern, diminishing ever closer to extinction. Moreover, the fact that their swelling population has spilled into Oregon's more vacant regions indicates that, aside from a few conflicts with livestock, there may be room for the animals."[5]

Beyond genetic testing, howling surveys, and tracking there is an entire suite of tools available to managers for monitoring and observing wolves. From the involvement of citizens making phone calls to report wolf activity to high-end GPS collars and radiotelemetry, these tools provide invaluable information managers can use to identify territories, estimate pack size, and anticipate conflict.

The OWP calls for a comprehensive monitoring program during the first stages of recovery that uses radiotelemetry collars to track and assess the state's wolves. As recovery progresses, monitoring will become less intensive, with the state relying on regular counts of wolf packs to monitor the population and reserving the placement of radio collars for special cases.

In 2002, David Mech and Shannon Barber wrote a critique of wildlife radio tracking in national parks.[6] At that point, they found the "potential for learning new information with [radio tracking] is almost unlimited." Radio tracking, which includes GPS, is used to gather information about an animal through signals sent by a device the animal carries. According to Mech, the technique is so "revolutionary that there is no other wildlife research technique that comes close to approximating its many benefits." Managers throughout the West have found this to be largely true. Once a single wolf in a pack is fitted with a transmitting collar, the ability to manage that pack increases almost exponentially. Without a collar, said Mech, managers are essentially blind to the movements and changes occurring within a pack or population. "Collaring is incredibly important for recovery in Oregon," said Morgan. "The plan makes a promise to delist in the future, and in order for that to happen we have to have as much information as possible about the population."

As of August 2012, thirteen wolves had been collared in Oregon—approximately 22 percent of the population—and Morgan and Roblyn Brown had barely taken a weekend off in more than four months. It seemed like every day throughout the West, wolves were demanding attention.

Context Clues

Oregon was the first state to receive naturally dispersing wolves from the northern Rocky Mountain population in Yellowstone and Idaho. It was also the first state to take a preemptive approach to managing wolves by creating a wolf management plan prior to the arrival of wolves in the state. That's where the firsts end, though.

From their relatively recent settling of Washington State to their comparatively long history in northern Montana, wolves have changed human and geographic landscapes across much of the western United States. The response they've generated has varied by location, but their impact can be widely seen in changes in legislation, animal husbandry practices, and public understanding of wildlife. In each state where wolves have established territory, the public and political reaction to their presence has been slightly different. Management practices and strategies have reflected the ideals and ideologies of the states, and the result has been the creation of an uneven tapestry of regulations and rules that spreads across the region. This hodgepodge of governance may fit the personalities of the societies in which it was created, but it fails to take into account animals that have no concept of state lines or governing authority.

Long before governing bodies began dissecting the issue of wolf management into state-sized chunks, the Roman poet Horace wrote, "It is your concern when your neighbor's wall is on fire."[1] While it has been easy to get wrapped up in the drama of Oregon's wolf-related struggles with descriptions of dead calves, wandering wolves, and close encounters, it is worthwhile to realize that Oregon is only one piece in the western wolf management puzzle. In order to see the whole picture, it's worth considering the management strategies of other western states.

Idaho

Under the Predator Control Act the last wolf in Idaho was thought to have been killed in the 1930s. When the USFWS signed the Northern Rocky Mountain Wolf Recovery Plan in the mid-1980s, Idaho was identified as prime recovery habitat, and an outline for the reintroduction of wolves into central Idaho was included in the plan. The recovery goal for the region, which included Yellowstone National Park in Montana, was thirty breeding pairs for three successive years. In January 1995, the federal government released fifteen wolves into central Idaho. The next year, twenty more were released, three packs were identified, and the first litter of pups was documented.

In 1998, the Idaho Legislative Wolf Oversight Committee began working on a management plan for the state. At that point the wolf population was estimated at 115 individuals with 10 breeding pairs. Four years later the plan was adopted by the state legislature. It identified Idaho Fish and Game as the primary agency responsible for wolf management once federal delisting occurred. Significant responsibility was also assigned to the Nez Perce Tribe. From 2002 to 2009, wolf management in Idaho vacillated between federal and state management as wolves were repeatedly delisted and relisted. Unlike Oregon, however, Idaho actively sought delisting and passed several legislative rulings that would increase the state's ability to lethally control for wolves once federal protection was removed. Of note, in May 2008 Idaho Fish and Game adopted a hunting season for wolves. A federal judge temporarily suspended the hunts in July, but the temperament of the state toward wolves had been made clear.

Shortly after a federal delisting of wolves in May 2009, Idaho declared open season on wolves. The state set a harvest limit of 220 wolves statewide and provided the public with information showing recent areas of wolf activity. In the first hunt, 188 wolf kills were reported. Protection then went back to the USFWS, and all wolf hunts in Idaho were suspended.

In response, Idaho governor C. L. "Butch" Otter wrote U.S. Secretary of the Interior Ken Salazar a letter terminating the state's role as a managing agent for the federal government's wolf programs. Otter wrote:

> *In Idaho, wolves serve as a constant reminder of how far we have strayed from the Founding Fathers' original intent of a national government with limited, enumerated powers bestowed by the states. Wolves were forced on Idaho in 1994 with no regard for the impacts the species would have on our people, wildlife and livestock. While some herald the introduction of wolves and the current population as a biological triumph, history will show that this program is a tragic example of oppressive, ham-handed "conservation" at its worst. Idahoans have suffered this intolerable situation for too long, but starting today at least the State no longer will be complicit.*

When the federal government made its final decision to delist wolves on May 5, 2011, Idaho Fish and Game resumed management of the state's wolf population and oversight of the Wolf Management Plan. The state's first action was to place wolf tags on sale. According to news reports, at the end of 2011, hunters had shot 255 wolves and trapped another 124. Biologists estimated the state still had 746 wolves and declared the 2012 hunting season open with no harvest limits. Wolf tags cost $11.50 for residents, an amount markedly less than a movie ticket and a bucket of popcorn.

Montana

The experience of reintroduction and reestablishment of wolves in Montana was similar to that of Idaho, with a few notable differences. Wolves dispersing from Canada began to repopulate northern Montana in the late 1980s. By 1993, there were an estimated forty-five wolves making up five packs in northwestern Montana. The 1995–1996 federal reintroduction brought another thirty-two wolves to the state.

Montana formed a citizen-based Wolf Management Advisory Council in 2000. The council was chaired by a rancher from Helena, Montana, and was charged with advising the state's wildlife agency in the creation of a wolf management plan that could be enacted once wolves were federally delisted. In 2001, the Montana legislature approved the state's management plan. By the time federal protections were removed from wolves in 2011, the plan had been revised numerous times. At the time of delisting it included strategies to reduce Montana's wolf population by 25 percent within a year. In order to achieve that goal, Montana also opened a hunting season on wolves. A harvest limit was set at 220 animals, but only 166 were killed during the 2011 hunting season. Managers were hoping for a more successful season in 2012 to bring the population down from the current 650 animals to about 450.

Washington

Wolves began establishing new packs in Washington through natural dispersal in 2008. The state Fish and Wildlife Commission approved a wolf management plan in December 2011. This plan follows Oregon's approach and has two major components. The first focuses on recovery objectives and strategies for removing wolves from Washington's Endangered Species List. The second addresses the need for strategies to manage conflict with livestock and big game herds.

Washington had the first major test of its management plan in the summer of 2012, when wolves in the state's northeast corner were involved in livestock attacks on public forest lands. The state wildlife department killed a nonbreeding female from the Wedge pack on August 7, 2012, after it confirmed the wolves had been involved in a July depredation that left one calf dead, five injured, and at least two missing. A second depredation occurred in the same area during the week of August 17, resulting in the death of another calf.

In response, the state sent a team of specialists into the area to attempt to capture and collar a member of the pack, and also to attempt the lethal removal of up to four other wolves. They were unsuccessful, and on August 31, the state reported two more calves were killed by wolves within the territory used by the Wedge pack. Efforts to remove the depredating wolves were increased, and on September 27, 2012, the state succeeded in eliminating the entire pack.

As of October 2012, Washington had seven confirmed wolf packs. One of the packs was in the state's southeast corner, and one was on the border of North Cascades National Park. The other five packs were in the northeast corner of the state. Based on surveys and genetic analysis, the state wildlife department believed wolves were dispersing into Washington from British Columbia and neighboring states.

Wyoming

In 2011, when the federal government officially removed gray wolves in the northern Rocky Mountain population from the Endangered Species List and granted managing authority to the states, there was an asterisk attached to the decision. According to the USFWS, Wyoming had failed to create an appropriate wolf management plan that would ensure the survival of the species, and because of that failure, wolves in Wyoming would continue to be managed by federal agents.

A year and a half later, it seemed the USFWS changed its opinion despite Wyoming's plan remaining the same. The federal agency began taking steps to hand control of Wyoming's wolves back to the state effective September 30, 2012. Like Idaho and Montana, Wyoming will need to maintain a population of 150 wolves and 15 breeding pairs to avoid relisting, but otherwise the state can manage how it sees fit.

There are currently 328 wolves in Wyoming according to the governor's office, and the state has already put regulations into effect that will classify wolves as predators beginning on October 1, 2012, which means that Wyoming hunters will be legally permitted to shoot the animals on sight at any time and for any reason. Hunting will not be allowed in Yellowstone National Park or Grand Teton National Park.

California

The only wolf currently confirmed in California is OR-7, but his presence has been enough to set the state thinking about creating a management plan and placing wolves under the protection of the state's Endangered Species Act. In August 2012, the California Department of Fish and Game recommended wolves be listed as endangered. The state's wildlife commission was scheduled to vote on the recommendation in October 2012.

Within the United States there are also populations of wolves in the Midwest and Southwest. These areas face their own challenges, and the states' respective governing agencies have created wolf management strategies that reflect the concerns and realities expressed within these regions. Unfortunately, there is no one area that can be held up as a bastion of perfect wolf management. However, it is possible for managers to learn from one another and for the public to evaluate their state's management decisions in light of their neighbors' plans.

Paul De Morgan, who facilitated the writing of both Oregon's and Washington's wolf management plans, said, "It's always possible that people's positions can change during the process through education and awareness building."

Wolves are new to almost every person living in the West. Learning to share the landscape with them has had, and will continue to have, a steep learning curve. Perhaps it can be softened through an increased mindfulness of the strategies and dramas currently underway in neighboring areas.

Moving Targets

My brake line cracked sometime between last night and this morning, but I found out only when I dropped into the Wallowa River canyon heading from La Grande to Joseph, Oregon. Feeling the brake pedal hit the floorboards, I downshifted from fifth to third before slamming it into second. At the bottom of the grade I pulled onto the shoulder and crawled under the chassis, where I found runny brake fluid coating the undercarriage and the inside of the driver's-side rear wheel like too much syrup poured over too-hot pancakes.

I limp the truck in to Enterprise, Oregon, and park. It's a Sunday. Monday is a holiday. There is not a single mechanic or auto parts store open. On my first-ever trip out to Wallowa County more than a decade ago, a high school kid leaned across a counter and told me, "Out here we change our own oil." As I lean against the side of the truck and watch the last of the brake fluid form a puddle around the tire, I think maybe I should move out here and get a little place with a garage. It's a thought that at the moment is born of exasperation and too many nights in a row spent howling at the moon, but it's also something I've been mulling over in general, and the reasons go far beyond having a place to work on the truck.

There aren't any stoplights in Wallowa County, Oregon. No McDonald's or Walmart sitting on the corner. No major airports or destination resorts, either. Where not narrowed by construction, landslides, or topography, the highways are two-lane and ruled by dust-covered American-made farm trucks with tumbleweeds stuck in their front grilles and herding dogs balanced on their heavy steel flatbeds. Narrow rivers snake along the bottom of steep forested canyons bearing native trout and returning Pacific salmon. Moose, cougars, black bears, and now wolves roam the side hills in relative obscurity. When the sun sets the whole Milky Way glitters and gleams in an inky black sky like sequins thrown by a three-year-old. It snows in June, sometimes in August. Old-timers say winter can last for nine months and that -20 degrees Fahrenheit isn't all that rare. They call it little Switzerland due in no small part to the Wallowa Mountains that jut into the air like sharp, pointed teeth.

The kid who years ago gave me advice on car maintenance probably came from a ranching family where he had been driving a truck during haying season since he could see over the steering wheel while sitting on a stack of phone books. He could probably not only perform basic automotive and farm equipment maintenance, but also butcher livestock and wild game, build fence, move irrigation lines, and back a trailer down a narrow, potholed canyon road without flinching. Born and bred in Enterprise, Oregon, population 1,934 and falling, he would have been well aware of what owning a cattle ranch in Wallowa County entailed; a whole lot of work and heartache. "Nobody out here has time to pat your hand and tell you not to worry. There's a lot to worry about, and always more to do," said rancher Rod Childers after telling me about all the work and worry that accompanies ranching in Wallowa County during modern times.

For more than a hundred years, Oregon families have been raising cattle and sheep on private farmland and public grazing lands in Oregon's northeast corner. In Wallowa, Grant, Baker, Union, Umatilla, and Morrow Counties, cows outnumber people by an average of three to one,[1] and agriculture, specifically the livestock industry, has consistently been a primary source of employment and income in the region. According to the Oregon Department of Agriculture, in 2011, sales of cows and calves from these six counties alone totaled upward of $16.5 million. Yet despite this, farm employment in the northeast region has experienced declines of more than 20 percent in the last twenty years, and nearly a third of farm owners have either sold their operations, retired, or gone out of business in the same time frame. "We're operating on such small profit margins out here that even a small loss, if repeated, can do in the business," said Childers.

The same can be said for the state's wolf population. Wolves were hunted to extinction in Oregon once, and it could happen again. There has to be a balance.

"Oregon is always going to have problems with wolves." I'm sitting in Dan Edge's university office. His bookshelves are filled with texts on wildlife management and biology. Students and other professors stop by randomly and poke their heads in the door to ask questions or drop off papers. We've been talking for twenty minutes, and Edge's Memphis, Tennessee, accent has gotten thicker as we've delved deeper into politics and conflict related to wolves. Soon his speech is dotted with small curses, but he's also chuckling, like the whole situation is darkly amusing. Maybe it is.

Oregon faces more inherent challenges related to wolf management than either Idaho or Montana in large part because it does not have the same quality or quantity of wilderness areas. Wolves in Oregon are largely going to be living in the areas between human settlements, said Edge. There's going to be conflict if only because of the proximity of people to wolves.

Though more than 50 percent of Oregon's land is federally owned and managed for the public by the Bureau of Land Management and the US Forest Service, it is largely divided into small, disconnected areas. In the areas that are contiguous, recreationists and ranchers with public lands grazing leases often compete with wildlife for space and resources. "Wolves are opportunistic predators," said Edge. "If their territory has them in the border country along private ranch property lines, or in areas where livestock are being let out to pasture for months at a time, it should not be a surprise that there are going to be some dead animals."

As a state, said Edge, Oregon needs to take steps to ensure a healthy wolf population despite divisive politics. "We need to do what needs to be done to get enough animals on the landscape so that wolves can be delisted," said Edge. "While they are under state protection, managers cannot do their jobs, the plan cannot be implemented, and conflict will continue." Even if we do nothing, adds Edge, if we just leave the wolves alone, we will have enough of a population to delist within ten years and possibly within five.

In 2008, Russ Morgan documented the first wolf pack in Oregon by the sound of howls filling the night. Since then, packs have come together in at least six different known locations around the state. The confirmed population count for wolves in Oregon in the last five years has gone from one to nearly fifty. Wolves in northeastern Oregon have been removed from federal protection. Pups have been born, and yes, livestock have been killed. The twenty-nine domestic animals that have been confirmed by the ODFW as wolf kills have perhaps done more than anything else to polarize the people of the state around the wolf issue. There is nothing trivial about those losses. However, to hold those depredations up as a sole reason for the wolf population to once again be destroyed by government mandate is to do the natural world a great injustice. All around the globe, every day, entire species are disappearing. In the majority of these cases there will never be an opportunity to make amends. Extinction is forever. Right now Oregon has been given a chance, not to change the past, but to create a new future.

When I started this project I thought I'd write a tidy overview of the wolf issue in Oregon. That was grossly naive. The wolf issue in Oregon is not a static, flat issue. It cannot be summed up and topped off with a nice thesis statement. It is a living, breathing organism with thousands of moving parts and it changes daily.

Repeatedly, as I spoke with people on all sides of the wolf issue, I was told, "The wolves are just being wolves." Whether it was a biologist or lawyer, a congressman or cattle rancher, "The wolves are just being wolves." When I called Morgan during the last days of my reporting and mentioned this, he chuckled a bit, and then repeated something he had said early on, "Yeah, it's the people that are the challenge."

Addendum

It took nearly two years but in mid-July 2013 the lawsuit filed in the Oregon Court of Appeals preventing the lethal removal of wolves by the Oregon Department of Fish and Wildlife was rendered moot when the Oregon Fish and Wildlife Commission adopted a series of new rules and provisions that amend the state's wolf management plan. The move came after a series of closed-door meetings in which conservation groups, the governor's office, the ODFW, and the livestock industry were able to reach an out-of-court agreement regarding the steps that must be taken by the industry and the state before lethal control of wolves can be instigated. According to the ODFW, the settlement makes the following key changes to the Oregon Wolf Plan:

• Requires that, before ODFW can use lethal control against wolves, it must confirm four qualifying incidents within a six-month time frame (the previous rule was two depredation incidents and no specific time frame).

• Requires the development and public disclosure of wolf-livestock conflict deterrence plans that identify non-lethal measures for implementation by landowners.

• Requires that these non-lethal measures be implemented by a landowner prior to a depredation for the depredation incident to count as one of the qualifying incidents for lethal control.

• Rules that any ODFW lethal control decision is valid for 45 days (the time frame was not previously standardized in rule; 45 days is consistent with what other western states have implemented).

"What we've done is hashed out something that is far from perfect but gives Oregon the most progressive wolf plan in the country," said Rob Klavins, a spokesperson for Oregon Wild, one of the groups involved in the original lawsuit. "With the new measures the state can only kill an endangered species at the request of an industry if there is undeniable evidence that nonlethal measures are being put in place and there are ongoing losses that can not be prevented."

As support for nonlethal management techniques, Klavins pointed to the fact that during the period in which the lawsuit was active the number of wolves in the state increased while the number of livestock kills attributable to wolves decreased. "With the easy option to kill wolves off the table, we saw livestock owners stepping up to the plate to prevent conflict from happening in the first place," he said.

That idea of livestock owners taking a more aggressive role in protecting their animals is a key component of the amendments to the plan. "The changes do not make it mandatory for livestock producers to use nonlethal measures to deter wolves; however, nonlethal measures must be in place if we are to qualify a livestock kill as a depredation," said state wolf coordinator Russ Morgan in response to the new rules. "The wolves aren't going to pay for somebody that is not willing to implement nonlethal measures to protect their livestock."

Oregon Governor John Kitzhaber signed off on the Commission's decision on July 19, 2013. The move made Oregon the only state in the west where killing wolves that attack livestock is a last resort, not a first option.

Appendix A

Time Line of Relevant Events

in the Reestablishment of Wolves in Oregon

1914 – Congress appropriates a small amount of funding for the control of predatory animals.

1915 – Congress allocates $125,000 for a biological survey focused on controlling predators.

1916 – An additional $75,000 is appropriated for predator control.

1920 – The Eradication Methods Laboratory is established in New Mexico and charged with determining methods of lethal control for predators. It is moved to Denver, Colorado, in 1921 and seven years later is renamed the Control Methods Research Laboratory.

March 2, 1931 – A congressional act provides federal authority for the control of mammalian predators, rodents, and birds.

1934 – The Division of Predatory Animal and Rodent Control is combined with law enforcement to form the Division of Game Management with a Section of Predator and Rodent Control.

1940 – The Control Methods Research Laboratory is combined with the Division of Food Studies to become the Branch of Wildlife Research.

1947 – The last known wolf in Oregon is killed.

1950s – Gray wolves have largely been extirpated from the lower forty-eight states under federal authorization.

1964 – The report *Predator and Rodent Control in the United States* is published. The report criticizes predator control as being "indiscriminate, nonselective, and excessive." It leads to minor, primarily administrative, changes in predator control, including another name change for the offices of predator control, which would now be known as the Division of Wildlife Services.

1973 – The Federal Endangered Species Act (ESA) is passed by the US Congress. According to the US Fish and Wildlife Service (USFWS), "the purpose of the ESA is to protect and recover imperiled species and the ecosystems upon which they depend. It is administered by the U.S. Fish and Wildlife Service and the Commerce Department's National Marine Fisheries Service."

1987 – The Oregon legislature enacts the state Endangered Species Act. The state's Endangered Species List includes all native species listed under federal protection as of May 15, 1987, plus any additional native species determined by the appropriate state agency to be in danger of extinction throughout any significant portion of its range within the state. The act's goal to conserve and protect species through "the use of methods and procedures necessary to bring a species to the point at which measures are no longer necessary" is similar to federal ESA goals.

1994 – The USFWS makes plans to reintroduce the gray wolf into Yellowstone National Park and areas of Montana and central Idaho. The wolves are to be classified as a nonessential experimental population under the federal ESA.

1995–1996 – The USFWS reintroduces sixty-six gray wolves to Yellowstone National Park and areas of Montana and central Idaho.

December 1998 – The estimated population of wolves in Idaho is 115. This is the first year that the goal of ten breeding pairs is attained.

January 1999 – B-45, a female gray wolf wearing a radio collar, disperses from Idaho to Oregon. She is captured and sent back to Idaho.

May 2000 – A wolf radio-collared in Idaho is killed by a vehicle on Interstate 84 outside Baker City, Oregon.

October 2000 – A male wolf is found shot to death between Ukiah and Pendleton, Oregon.

September 2001 – The USFWS documents thirty pairs of wolves in the three-state area of Idaho, Montana, and Wyoming, triggering the three-year countdown to delisting as called for under the federal ESA and the wolf management plan.

2002–2003 – The Oregon Fish and Wildlife Commission initiates a process in 2002 to educate itself and the public about wolf issues and to enable the agency to be prepared and proactive for wolves' arrival in Oregon. The process includes fifteen town hall meetings in late 2002 and early 2003.

April 2003 – The Oregon Department of Fish and Wildlife (ODFW) requests nomination for members to participate on the Wolf Advisory Committee with the goal of creating a conservation and management plan for the state.

November 2003 – The first meeting of Oregon's Wolf Advisory Committee is held at Silver Falls State Park.

September 9, 2004 – Oregon's Wolf Advisory Committee submits a draft of the Oregon Wolf Conservation and Management Plan to the state Fish and Wildlife Commission.

November 2004–February 2005 – Public comment period for Oregon's draft wolf plan is held. More than two thousand comments are submitted to the state.

February 11, 2005 – Oregon officially adopts the state management plan for wolves.

February 8, 2007 – Notice of federal delisting process is published in the *Federal Register*. Delisting is proposed in Idaho, Montana, Wyoming, and parts of Washington, Oregon, and Utah. Delisting may proceed without Wyoming.

January 2008 – B-300, a collared female wolf from Idaho, is confirmed to be in northeast Oregon.

February 27, 2008 – The USFWS federal delisting rule is posted in the *Federal Register*.

March 28, 2008 – The federal delisting rule becomes final. In Idaho and Montana wolves will be managed as a big game animal and subjected to hunting seasons. The USFWS will continue to monitor wolf recovery for five years.

April 28, 2008 – Twelve conservation and animal rights groups file a lawsuit in federal court challenging the USFWS's decision to remove the gray wolf in Idaho and the northern Rocky Mountains from the Endangered Species List and request a preliminary injunction staying the delisting until the lawsuit is settled.

July 18, 2008 – A federal district judge issues a preliminary injunction that returns wolves in Idaho to endangered species protection and puts hunting seasons on hold.

July 21, 2008 – ODFW biologists confirm the first pack in Oregon when they hear the howls of at least two adults and several pups in Union County.

October 14, 2008 – A federal court grants the United States' motion to return the delisting rule to the USFWS. The lawsuit that challenged the delisting is also dismissed.

January 12, 2009 – The USFWS submits to the *Federal Register* the final rule to identify the northern Rocky Mountain population of gray wolves as a distinct population segment and to revise the list of endangered and threatened wildlife.

January 14, 2009 – The USFWS announces the pending publication of a delisting rule for gray wolves in the northern Rocky Mountains and western Great Lakes. The Northern Rockies rule, however, does not include Wyoming, where wolves will remain on the Endangered Species List.

January 20, 2009 – The Obama administration suspends the proposed delisting rule for the northern Rocky Mountain population until a review can occur.

March 6, 2009 – US interior secretary Ken Salazar announces the USFWS will send the delisting rule to the *Federal Register* for publication. The rule is to take effect days after publication and includes all wolves in the northern Rocky Mountain population with the exception of those in Wyoming.

April 2, 2009 – The USFWS rule delisting gray wolves in the northern Rockies and western Great Lakes is published in the *Federal Register*.

April 9–13, 2009 – The first livestock depredations by wolves in Oregon occur in the Keating Valley outside Baker City. Twenty-nine animals, mostly lambs, are killed. A variety of nonlethal preventive measures are incorporated into ranch management in the area.

May 4, 2009 – A male gray wolf suspected in the Keating Valley depredations is captured, collared, and released by the ODFW. A smaller female wolf is also identified. The USFWS rule delisting gray wolves in the northern Rockies and western Great Lakes becomes official. Oregon is given management control of wolves.

June 2009 – A legal challenge is filed against the USFWS's decision to remove federal protection of gray wolves.

September 1, 2009 – The first regulated wolf hunt in Idaho opens.

September 5, 2009 – After two more depredation incidents in the Keating Valley, the ODFW kills the two wolves involved in the livestock attacks.

November 2009 – B-300 is observed with nine other wolves, including pups, in the Imnaha area outside Joseph, Oregon. The Imnaha pack is confirmed.

February 2010 – Three additional members of the Imnaha pack are captured
and radio-collared by the ODFW, including the alpha male, which is fitted
with a GPS collar that stores location information every six hours.

March 26, 2010 – Members of the Imnaha pack are found within a small fenced
cow pasture near a ranch house and successfully hazed away by landowners.

May 5–June 4, 2010 – Wolves from the Imnaha pack kill six calves at area
ranches. The ODFW authorizes USDA Wildlife Services to kill two wolves from
the pack in an effort to disrupt the depredation cycle.

June 29, 2010 – The ODFW files a temporary rule change with the secretary of
state's office that changes the language guiding lethal responses to wolf
livestock depredation, making it easier for the state to remove depredating
wolves.

July 12, 2010 – Four environmental groups file a lawsuit against the ODFW in
State Circuit Court alleging that the ODFW violated the state Endangered
Species Act, Oregon administrative rules, and the Administrative Procedures
Act when it authorized lethal removal of wolves.

July 14, 2010 – A camera captures an image confirming at least four new pups
for the Imnaha pack.

August 4, 2010 – The ODFW captures and collars a male wolf from the Wenaha
pack.

August 5, 2010 – Gray wolves in Idaho and the northern Rocky Mountains are
returned to endangered species status. US district court judge Donald Molloy
rules that the USFWS's delisting rule does not comply with the Endangered
Species Act.

August 20, 2010 – The ODFW captures two pups from the Wenaha pack,
confirming that the pack successfully reproduced.

October 8, 2010 – The male wolf captured on August 4, 2010, by the ODFW is
found dead in Union County. The USFWS opens an investigation into the
possible poaching.

December 23, 2010 – Trail cameras confirm at least one pup for the Wenaha
pack.

January 2011 – The ODFW finds evidence of a new wolf pack in the Walla Walla
drainage on the Oregon-Washington border.

March 1, 2011 – The ODFW reports capturing and collaring three wolves from
the Imnaha pack.

March 2, 2011 – A wolf from the Imnaha pack is found dead.

April 15, 2011 – Congress passes the federal budget, which includes a rider requiring the USFWS to republish the 2009 delisting rule within sixty days and to remove wolves in Montana, Idaho, eastern Washington, eastern Oregon, and north-central Utah from the Endangered Species List.

May 5, 2011 – The USFWS publishes a rule removing wolves in the northern Rocky Mountain population from federal protection, with the exception of wolves in Wyoming. Wolf tags go on sale in Idaho and Montana.

May 10, 2011 – The ODFW makes plan to kill two wolves from the Imnaha pack involved in chronic depredation. Also, eight "caught-in-the-act" permits are issued to area ranchers.

May 16, 2011 – A dead calf in the Imanha territory is confirmed as a wolf kill.

May 17, 2011 – The ODFW captures and kills a young male wolf from the Imnaha pack.

May 19, 2011 – A young female wolf from the Imnaha pack is shot by state agents. The alpha male from the Imnaha pack is captured and fitted with a new GPS collar.

June 6, 2011 – Another calf is confirmed as a wolf kill in the Imnaha territory.

August 2011 – ODFW employees confirm at least one pup for the Imnaha pack and four adults in the Wenaha pack.

August 3, 2011 – Governor Kitzhaber signs into law House Bill 3560, authorizing the state to give compensation to ranchers suffering depredation or costs associated with implementing nonlethal measures to prevent wolf attacks. The act is funded by $100,000 from the state general fund.

August 11, 2011 – Trail camera footage shows two wolves from the Walla Walla pack in Umatilla County, Oregon.

August 22, 2011 – A lone wolf is documented in the Mount Emily area outside La Grande, Oregon.

September 2011 – OR-7 leaves the Imnaha pack and is sighted in Baker County, Oregon.

September 23, 2011 – After another calf depredation, the ODFW makes plans to kill the alpha male and an uncollared yearling from the Imnaha pack. This would decrease the Imnaha pack to two members.

September 26, 2011 – The ODFW confirms at least two pups for the Walla Walla pack.

October 2011 – The ODFW captures and collars two wolves from the Walla Walla pack.

October 5, 2011 – The Oregon Court of Appeals grants a temporary injunction in a legal case brought by three conservation groups against the ODFW to prevent the killing of wolves in the Imnaha pack.

October 11, 2011 – The ODFW confirms another livestock loss by depredating wolves in the Imnaha territory.

October 24, 2011 – The ODFW confirms a new wolf pack comprising at least five animals in the Snake River drainage in northeastern Oregon.

November 14, 2011 – The Oregon Court of Appeals extends the ban on the lethal removal of wolves in Oregon indefinitely.

December 13, 2011 – The ODFW confirms another livestock loss by depredating wolves in the Imnaha territory.

December 29, 2011 – OR-7 enters California.

January 7–14, 2012 – The ODFW confirms another livestock loss by depredating wolves in the Imnaha territory. Two more losses are classified as probable kills.

February 23, 2012 – House Bill 4158, submitted and backed by the Oregon Cattlemen's Association and clarifying the state's authorization to kill wolves, passes in the House.

March 5, 2012 – Oregon's House Bill 4158, nicknamed the "kill bill," dies in the Senate.

March 8, 2012 – The ODFW confirms depredation of three cows by wolves of the Imnaha pack.

April 2, 2012 – The ODFW captures and collars a black wolf thought to be the alpha male from the Wenaha pack.

June 11, 2012 – The ODFW captures and collars a female wolf from the Wenaha pack.

June 20, 2012 – The ODFW captures and collars a male wolf in the Mount Emily area outside La Grande, Oregon.

July 26, 2012 – The ODFW confirms another livestock loss by depredating wolves in the Imnaha territory.

August 1, 2012 – The ODFW confirms at least six pups for the Imnaha pack and at least three pups for the Snake River pack. Genetic tests of two collared wolves in the Walla Walla pack show they are not related to any other wolves in Oregon.

August 2, 2012 – The ODFW captures and collars a young male wolf pup in the Snake River pack. This first wolf of the pack to be fitted with a collar will enable the tracking and monitoring of the group.

August 10, 2012 – The ODFW confirms two pups from the Walla Walla pack. There are now at least ten animals in the pack, eight adults and two pups.

August 15, 2012 – The ODFW confirms seven pups for the Wenaha pack, as well as a new wolf pack in the Umatilla River area comprising at least two adults and two pups.

August 30, 2012 – The ODFW confirms a new wolf pack in the Upper Minam River area in northeastern Oregon. The pack comprises at least two adults and five pups. Another wolf was captured in a nearby area earlier in the summer, but it is unknown if she is part of the pack.

August 31–September 3, 2012 – The ODFW confirms two livestock depredations by wolves in the Imnaha pack and classifies a third as probable.

Appendix B

2010 Revisions to the Oregon Wolf Conservation
and Management Plan

The Oregon Wolf Conservation and Management Plan (OWP) is subject to review every five years by the state's Fish and Wildlife Commission. The first review of the OWP in 2010 incorporated stakeholder input collected during meetings with the following fourteen groups:

Baker County Natural Resources Advisory Committee
Defenders of Wildlife
Hells Canyon Preservation Council
Nez Perce Tribe
Oregon Cattlemen's Association
Oregon Department of Agriculture
Oregon Farm
Oregon Hunters
Oregon Wild
Oregon Wool Growers Association

Umatilla Tribe

United States Department of Agriculture, Wildlife Services

United States Fish and Wildlife Service

United States Forest Service

Each meeting focused on identifying what parts of the OWP had worked well and what parts of the plan needed improvement. As was the case in the original drafting of the plan, stakeholder input was diverse and often contradictory. The majority of input received at all meetings was related to managing wolf-livestock conflict. Discussions were held around the following ten policy issues:

1. Are the existing criteria for initiating ODFW-authorized lethal taking of depredating wolves adequate to protect livestock while conserving wolves?
2. Is the current wolf relocation and translocation section of the plan adequate?
3. Are the wolf population objectives and delisting criteria adequate?
4. In cases of suspected wolf depredation of livestock, who should confirm losses of wolf-killed livestock?
5. Is the current caught-in-the-act lethal permit system adequate for addressing wolf depredation?
6. Should control measures for wolf-livestock conflicts be applied to pets and residences?
7. Should the plan mandate disease testing of Oregon wolves?
8. Should the plan continue to call for compensation of wolf-caused losses of livestock, working dogs, or sporting dogs?
9. Regarding wolf-livestock conflicts, should the plan contain different wolf management principles on public versus private lands?
10. Are nonlethal or preventive efforts for addressing wolf-livestock conflicts as currently stated in the plan adequate for protecting livestock and wolves?

From the responses to these questions, the ODFW made numerous changes to clarify the language of the plan. In addition, changes to the plan included the addition of county officials as contact options for landowners in the event of suspected depredation; a clarification of the circumstances under which "caught-in-the-act" permits may be given to land owners; and the addition of language specifying that preventive measures taken by livestock producers prior to actual wolf conflict will count toward the ODFW authorizing harassment or lethal take permits.

The state Fish and Wildlife Commission adopted the revisions to the OWP on October 1, 2010.

Appendix C

Online Administrative Documents

The Oregon Department of Fish and Wildlife wolf pages:
   http://www.dfw.state.or.us/wolves/
The Oregon Wolf Conservation and Management Plan:
   http://www.dfw.state.or.us/Wolves/management_plan.asp
United States Fish and Wildlife Service information on Gray Wolves:
   http://www.fws.gov/mountain-prairie/species/mammals/wolf/
Cascadia Wildlands, Center for Biological Diversity, and Oregon Wild v. Department of Fish and Wildlife and Fish and Wildlife Commission and The Oregon Cattlemen's Association: Court of Appeals No. A149672: Order Staying Enforcement of Rule Pending Judicial Review:
   www.publications.ojd.state.or.us/Publications/A149672order.pdf

Acknowledgments

Wolves are not an easy subject in the West, and I am deeply grateful for the many good men and women who chose to wade into the torrent of information and issues to share in the creation of this book. Without Russ Morgan at the Oregon Department of Fish and Wildlife I would have never gotten off the ground, or into the field. He has an incredibly difficult job, and his willingness to share his experiences and expertise in the name of better education leaves me long in his debt. Also of the ODFW, Roblyn Brown, Craig Ely, Michelle Tate, Colleen Munson, and Michelle Dennehy were all instrumental in providing insight and access to information. Dan Edge, formerly of the ODFW Wildlife Commission, provided honest evaluation of the processes behind wolf management. The members of the ranching and conservation communities who took part in this project showed great faith, and specifically I would like to thank Rod Childers for opening the first doors and Rob Klavins for all his follow-up. A number of scientists and researchers were invaluable in providing the details and explanations of their work, including Tabitha Viner and Lisette Waits. Tabitha, thank you for not flinching when I asked for all the gory details. Mary Elizabeth Braun, acquisitions editor at OSU Press, believed in this book before the first word was written, and throughout the process she served as a sounding board, a friend, and a relentless editor. It wouldn't have happened without her. For their editing expertise and support I also thank Jo Alexander and Laurel Anderton, and for her honest reviews, Sharman Apt Russell, who long ago told me to play my strengths. Matt and Seonaid

Eaton and the entire Eaton family provided support, business expertise, and a warm, loving place to write. They were there when the book started and when the writing ended, and I am so glad. Thank you to my parents, Mark and Danielle, for their love, and to Lindsay Miller, who put her life on hold to help me with mine. Finally, and with everything I have, thank you to Mike Eaton. He believed every step of the way and never wavered in his support or love. I am very lucky.

Notes

Wolves in Oregon

1   In Minnesota, gray wolves were listed as threatened, not endangered.
2   Under the Northern Rocky Mountain Wolf Recovery Plan, a wolf pack is a group of wolves, usually consisting of a male, female, and their offspring. A breeding pair is considered two wolves of the opposite sex and adequate age, capable of producing offspring. This differs from the Oregon Wolf Plan, which defines a pack as four or more wolves traveling together in winter, and a breeding pair as an adult male and female with at least two pups at the end of the year.
3   L. David Mech and Luigi Boitani, eds., *Wolves: Behavior, Ecology, and Conservation* (Chicago: University of Chicago Press, 2003), 11.
4   Oregon created its own Endangered Species Act and listed the gray wolf as endangered in 1987.
5   Uncharacteristically for sexually mature gray wolves, B-45 and her mate did not produce pups in 2000 or 2001. Source: Curt M. Mack, Isaac Babcock, and Jim Holyan, *Idaho Wolf Recovery Program: Restoration and Management of Gray Wolves in Idaho, Progress Report 1999–2001* (Lapwai, ID: Nez Perce Tribe, Department of Wildlife Management, 2002).
6   Rolf O. Peterson and Paolo Ciucci, "The Wolf as Carnivore," in *Wolves: Behavior, Ecology and Conservation* (Chicago: University of Chicago Press, 2003), 104–30.

First Meetings

1   A sixty-pound golden retriever has a front foot about two and a half inches long by about two inches wide.
2   Morgan identified the pups' sex based on observable physical characteristics, which included the spacing between their ears.
3   During the course of plan development, two committee members were replaced due to other obligations that took precedence over their participation: Bret Michalski, Bend, OR, replaced Dan Edge, and Meg Mitchell was replaced by Kurt Wiedenmann, La Grande, OR.

4   In 2003, Portland had a population of 539,546, while little Ione, Oregon, weighed in with 329 people.

Making the Plan

1   I spoke at length with De Morgan, Ely, and Henjum about the politics that went on before and during WAC meetings. All parties agreed that there were one or two committee members who came to the table unwilling to work collaboratively; however, De Morgan and the ODFW employees were reticent to name names lest they should appear in print. This was in line with the associated guidelines that suggested individuals involved in the planning process avoid finger-pointing and singling others out.

2   The plan undergoes a formal review every five years, at which time revisions can be made. See Appendix B for notes on 2010 revisions.

Depredation

1   Up until May 2011 wolves in all of Oregon were protected under both the state and federal Endangered Species Acts. On May 5, wolves in the northeast corner of the state were removed from federal protection, but they remained on the state list.

2   This goes a long way toward explaining why the process of writing the plan was so important, and also so onerous.

3   L. David Mech, "The Challenge and Opportunity of Recovering Wolf Populations," *Conservation Biology* 9, no. 2 (1995): 270–78.

4   Mech and Boitani, *Wolves: Behavior, Ecology, and Conservation*.

5   Ibid., 123.

6   Ibid., 306.

7   L. David Mech, *The Wolf: The Ecology and Behavior of an Endangered Species* (Garden City, NY: Natural History Press, 1970).

8   Mech and Boitani, *Wolves: Behavior, Ecology, and Conservation*, 120.

9   The female wolf was found dead on March 1, 2011. Her carcass was transported to Washington State University Veterinary Diagnostic Laboratory for a complete examination. The carcass had no visible indication of foul play or any other cause of death.

10 In 2005, when the OWP was written, gray wolves were protected under the federal and state ESAs. From 2005 to 2009, Oregon managed wolves under the OWP by proxy for the USFWS. However, certain aspects of the plan, specifically the lethal removal of wolves due to chronic depredation, could not be implemented due to the confines of the federal ESA. In 2009, wolves in the northern Rocky Mountain population area, which includes the northeast corner of Oregon, were briefly removed from federal protection. This delisting coincided with the Keating Valley depredations and the subsequent killing of

those wolves by the ODFW. In August 2010, the decision to remove the northern Rocky Mountain population from federal protection was struck down in court and wolves were once again listed under the federal ESA. On May 5, 2011, the USFWS issued a final ruling to remove all federal protections for the wolves in the northern Rocky Mountain population. Management authority was given immediately to the states, with the exception of Wyoming, where wolves would remain under federal protection.

Litigation

1   The original case was between the petitioners Cascadia Wildlands, Center for Biological Diversity, and Oregon Wild, with the ODFW as the respondent. The Oregon Cattlemen's Association inserted itself into the case on the grounds that if the ODFW lost, the OCA would suffer harm because wolves would kill cattle.
2   All cattle and calves in Oregon as of January 1, 2011, totaled 1.33 million head, 6 percent above the 1.26 million on January 1, 2010. Of those animals, 55,000 died before being sold. Less than 0.1 percent of those deaths could be attributed to wolves.

The Problems of Retribution

1   A standard credit card is about one millimeter thick. Stack five together and the height of the stack when the cards are set horizontally is about the width of a bullet wound like the one Viner described.
2   Russ Morgan, personal communication.

The Media Circus

1   According to the Oregon Wild website, the finalists were: Journey, submitted by a seven-year-old girl in Mountain Home, Idaho, and an eleven-year-old in Dickinson, North Dakota; Arthur, from a thirteen-year-old in Finland; Lupin, from a thirteen-year-old in La Grande, Oregon; Max, suggested three times, from a sixth-grade class in North Clackamas, Oregon, from a second grader in Saint Paul, Minnesota, and from a second grader in Eugene, Oregon; and Takota, from a fourteen-year-old in Oklahoma.
2   Mech and Boitani, *Wolves: Behavior, Ecology, and Conservation*, 298.
3   Ibid., 297.
4   Ibid., 295.
5   Ibid., 298.

The Science of Recovery

1   This is true of all organisms. Plants, fungi, and humans all rely on habitat and genetic variation to keep going as species. It's part of why incest, especially over generations, is less than a good idea.

2   Adam R. Boyko, "The Domestic Dog: Man's Best Friend in the Genomic Era," *Genome Biology* 12 (2011): 216.

3   B. M. von Holdt, D. R. Stahler, E. E. Bangs, D. W. Smith, M. D. Jiminez, C. M. Mack,C. C. Niemeyer,J. P. Pollinger,and R. K. Wayne, "A Novel Assessment of Population Structure and Gene Flow in Grey Wolf Populations of the Northern Rocky Mountains of the United States," *Molecular Ecology* 19(20) (2010): 4412–27.

4   Mech and Boitani, *Wolves: Behavior, Ecology, and Conservation*, 164.

5   "Wolves Are Returning to Oregon—But Not All Locals Want Them," Smithsonian Institution, August 31, 2012, http://blogs.smithsonianmag.com/adventure/2012/08/wolves-are-returning-to-oregon-but-not-all-locals-want-them/.

6   L. David Mech and Shannon M. Barber, "A Critique of Wildlife Radio-tracking and Its Use in National Parks: A Report to the U.S. National Park Service," (Jamestown, ND: Northern Prairie Wildlife Research Center Online, 2002), http://www.npwrc.usgs.gov/resource/wildlife/radiotrk/index.htm.

Context Clues

1   Actually, he wrote something much more akin to *Nam tua res agitur, paries cum proximus ardet.* Epistles book 1, epistle 18, line 84.

Moving Targets

1   Human population numbers from "Annual Estimates of the Resident Population for Counties of Oregon: April 1, 2010 to July 1, 2011 (CO-EST2011-01-41)." Source: U.S. Census Bureau, Population Division. Cattle population numbers from USDA/NASS (National Agricultural Statistics Service) and other government reports, 2010.

Index